Q: Skills for Success

READING AND WRITING

1

Lawrence Lawson

OXFORD
UNIVERSITY PRESS

OXFORD
UNIVERSITY PRESS

198 Madison Avenue
New York, NY 10016 USA

Great Clarendon Street, Oxford ox2 6dp UK

Oxford University Press is a department of the University of Oxford.
It furthers the University's objective of excellence in research, scholarship,
and education by publishing worldwide in

Oxford New York

Auckland Cape Town Dar es Salaam Hong Kong Karachi
Kuala Lumpur Madrid Melbourne Mexico City Nairobi
New Delhi Shanghai Taipei Toronto

With offices in

Argentina Austria Brazil Chile Czech Republic France Greece
Guatemala Hungary Italy Japan Poland Portugal Singapore
South Korea Switzerland Thailand Turkey Ukraine Vietnam

OXFORD and OXFORD ENGLISH are registered trademarks of
Oxford University Press.

General Manager, American ELT: Laura Pearson
Publisher: Stephanie Karras
Associate Publishing Manager: Sharon Sargent
Associate Development Editor: Keyana Shaw
Director, ADP: Susan Sanguily
Executive Design Manager: Maj-Britt Hagsted
Associate Design Manager: Michael Steinhofer
Electronic Production Manager: Julie Armstrong
Production Artist: Elissa Santos
Cover Design: Michael Steinhofer
Production Coordinator: Elizabeth Matsumoto

ISBN: 978-0-19-475627-3 Reading and Writing 1 Teacher's Handbook Pack
ISBN: 978-0-19-475652-5 Reading and Writing 1 Teacher's Handbook
ISBN: 978-0-19-475664-8 Reading and Writing 1 Testing Program CD-ROM
ISBN: 978-0-19-475643-3 Q Online Practice Teacher Access Code Card

Printed in China

This book is printed on paper from certified and well-managed sources.

10 9 8 7 6 5 4

ACKNOWLEDGMENTS

*The publisher would like to thank the following for their kind permission to reproduce
photographs:*
p. vi Marcin Krygier/iStockphoto; xiii Rüstem GÜRLER/iStockphoto

CONTENTS

WELCOME TO **Q**:Skills for Success

Q: Skills for Success is a six-level series with two strands,
Reading and Writing and *Listening and Speaking*.

READING AND WRITING

LISTENING AND SPEAKING

WITH Q ONLINE PRACTICE

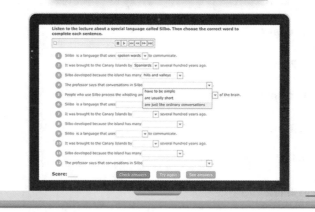

To the Teacher

Highlights of the *Q: Skills for Success* Teacher's Handbook

As you probably know from your own teaching experience, students want to know the point of a lesson. They want to know the "why" even when they understand the "how." In the classroom, the "why" is the learning outcome, and to be successful, students need to know it. The learning outcome provides a clear reason for classroom work and helps students meaningfully access new material.

Each unit in Oxford's *Q: Skills for Success* series builds around a thought-provoking question related to that unit's unique learning outcome. Students learn vocabulary to answer the unit question; consider new information related to the unit's theme that utilizes this vocabulary; use this information to think critically about new questions; and use those answers to practice the new reading, vocabulary, grammar, and writing skills they need to achieve the unit's learning outcome.

Each aspect of the learning process in the Q series builds toward completing the learning outcome. This interconnected process of considering new information is at the heart of a critical thinking approach and forms the basis of the students' work in each unit of the Q series. At the end of the unit, students complete a practical project built around the learning outcome.

Learning outcomes create expectations in the classroom: expectations of what students will learn, what teachers will teach, and what lessons will focus on. Students benefit because they know they need to learn content for a purpose; teachers benefit because they can plan activities that reinforce the knowledge and skills students need to complete the learning outcome. In short, learning outcomes provide the focus that lessons need.

In this example unit, students are asked to think about and discuss what makes them laugh.

The unit assignment ties into that unit's unique learning outcome.

UNIT 6

Unit QUESTION
What makes you laugh?

Laughter

READING • identifying the topic sentence in a paragraph
VOCABULARY • using the dictionary
GRAMMAR • sentences with *when*
WRITING • writing a topic sentence

LEARNING OUTCOME
Explain what makes you or someone you know laugh.

Writing a Paragraph	20 points	15 points	10 points	0 points
The first line of the paragraph is indented, and the paragraph has an appropriate topic sentence.				
Sentences with *when* and *because* are correct.				
Paragraph explains what makes someone laugh using vocabulary from the unit.				
Sentences begin with capital letters and end with appropriate punctuation.				
Every sentence has a subject and a verb and they are in agreement.				

Total points: _____
Comments:

Clear assessments allow both teachers and students to comment on and measure learner outcomes.

▶ *Reading and Writing 1, page 116*

Q Unit Assignment: Write a paragraph about what makes someone laugh

Unit Question (5 minutes)

Refer students back to the ideas they discussed at the beginning of the unit about laughter. Ask: *What makes you or someone you know laugh?* Bring out the answers students wrote on poster paper at the beginning of the unit. Cue students if necessary by asking specific questions about the content of the unit: *Why is laughter important? What makes you laugh the hardest? What kinds of things do you find funny? What kinds of things are not funny?* Read the direction lines for the assignment together to ensure understanding.

Learning Outcome

1. Tie the Unit Assignment to the unit learning outcome. Say: *The outcome for this unit is to explain what makes you or someone you know laugh. This Unit Assignment is going to let you show your skill at writing paragraphs, using a topic sentence, and with when and because*

CRITICAL THINKING

A critical thinking approach asks students to process new information and to learn how to apply that information to a new situation. Teachers might set learning outcomes to give students targets to hit—for example: "After this lesson, give three reasons why people immigrate"—and the materials and exercises in the lesson provide students with the knowledge and skills to think critically and discover *their* three reasons.

Questions are important catalysts in the critical thinking process. Questions encourage students to reflect on and apply their knowledge to new situations. Students and teachers work together to understand, analyze, synthesize, and evaluate the lesson's questions and content to reach the stated outcomes. As students become more familiar with these stages of the critical thinking process, they will be able to use new information to complete tasks more efficiently and in unique and meaningful ways.

Tip Critical Thinking

In Activity B, you have to **restate**, or say again in perhaps a different way, some of the information you learned in the two readings. **Restating** is a good way to review information.

B (10 minutes)

1. Introduce the Unit Question, *Why do people immigrate to other countries?* Ask related information questions or questions about personal experience to help students prepare for answering the more abstract unit question: *Did you immigrate to this country? What were your reasons for leaving your home country? What were your reasons for choosing your new country? What did you bring with you?*

2. Tell students: *Let's start off our discussion by listing reasons why people might immigrate. For example, we could start our list with* finding work *because many people look for jobs in new countries. But there are many other reasons why people immigrate. What else can we think of?*

Throughout the Student Book, *Critical Thinking Tips* accompany certain activities, helping students to practice and understand these critical thinking skills.

Critical Thinking Tip (1 minute)

1. Read the tip aloud.

2. Tell students that restating also helps to ensure that they have understood something correctly. After reading a new piece of information, they should try to restate it to a classmate who has also read the information, to ensure that they both have the same understanding of information.

The *Q Teacher's Handbook* features notes offering questions for expanded thought and discussion.

CRITICAL Q EXPANSION ACTIVITIES

The *Q Teacher's Handbook* expands on the critical thinking approach with the Critical Q Expansion Activities. These activities allow teachers to facilitate more practice for their students. The Critical Q Expansion Activities supplement the *Q Student Book* by expanding on skills and language students are practicing.

In today's classrooms, it's necessary that students have the ability to apply the skills they have learned to new situations with materials they have never seen before. *Q*'s focus on critical thinking and the *Q Teacher's Handbook*'s emphasis on practicing critical thinking skills through the Critical Q Expansion Activities prepares students to excel in this important skill.

The easy-to-use activity suggestions increase student practice and success with critical thinking skills.

Critical Q: Expansion Activity

Outlining

1. Explain to students: *A popular way to prepare to outline one's ideas is to use a cluster map. In a cluster map, a big circle is drawn in the middle of a page or on the board, and a main point is written inside it—**this will become the topic sentence in the outline.***

2. Then explain: *Next, lines are drawn away from the circle and new, smaller circles are attached to the other end of those lines. Inside each of the smaller circles, ideas are written which relate to the main point—**these become supporting sentences in the outline.***

21ST CENTURY SKILLS

Both the academic and professional worlds are becoming increasingly interdependent. The toughest problems are solved only when looked at from multiple perspectives. Success in the 21st century requires more than just core academic knowledge—though that is still crucial. Now, successful students have to collaborate, innovate, adapt, be self-directed, be flexible, be creative, be tech-literate, practice teamwork, and be accountable—both individually and in groups.

Q approaches language learning in light of these important 21st Century Skills. Each unit asks students to practice many of these attributes, from collaboration to innovation to accountability, *while* they are learning new language and content. The *Q Student Books* focus on these increasingly important skills with unique team, pair, and individual activities. Additionally, the *Q Teacher's Handbooks* provide support with easy-to-use 21st Century Skill sections for teachers who want to incorporate skills like "openness to other people's ideas and opinions" into their classrooms but aren't sure where to start.

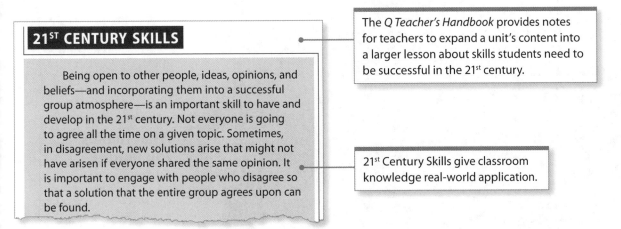

21ST CENTURY SKILLS

Being open to other people, ideas, opinions, and beliefs—and incorporating them into a successful group atmosphere—is an important skill to have and develop in the 21st century. Not everyone is going to agree all the time on a given topic. Sometimes, in disagreement, new solutions arise that might not have arisen if everyone shared the same opinion. It is important to engage with people who disagree so that a solution that the entire group agrees upon can be found.

The *Q Teacher's Handbook* provides notes for teachers to expand a unit's content into a larger lesson about skills students need to be successful in the 21st century.

21st Century Skills give classroom knowledge real-world application.

Q ONLINE PRACTICE

Q Online Practice is an online workbook that gives students quick access to all-new content in a range of additional practice activities. The interface is intuitive and user-friendly, allowing students to focus on enhancing their language skills.

For the teacher, *Q Online Practice* includes a digital grade book providing immediate and accurate assessment of each student's progress. Straightforward individual student or class reports can be viewed onscreen, printed, or exported, giving you comprehensive feedback on what students have mastered or where they need more help.

Teacher's Access Code Cards for the digital grade book are available upon adoption or for purchase. Use the access code to register for your *Q Online Practice* account at www.Qonlinepractice.com.

These features of the *Q: Skills for Success* series enable you to help your students develop the skills they need to succeed in their future academic and professional careers. By using learning outcomes, critical thinking, and 21st century skills, you help students gain a deeper knowledge of the material they are presented with, both in and out of the classroom.

Q connects critical thinking, language skills, and learning outcomes.

LANGUAGE SKILLS

Explicit skills instruction enables students to meet their academic and professional goals.

LEARNING OUTCOMES

Clearly identified **learning outcomes** focus students on the goal of their instruction.

UNIT 6
Laughter

READING	identifying the topic sentence in a paragraph
VOCABULARY	using the dictionary
GRAMMAR	sentences with *when*
WRITING	writing a topic sentence

LEARNING OUTCOME
Explain what makes you or someone you know laugh.

Unit QUESTION

What makes you laugh?

PREVIEW THE UNIT

A Discuss these questions with your classmates.
Do you laugh often?
What kind of laugh do you have? Is it loud or quiet?
Look at the photo. Why are the women laughing?

B Discuss the Unit Question above with your classmates.

Listen to *The Q Classroom*, Track 2 on CD 2, to hear other answers.

100   UNIT 6

101

CRITICAL THINKING

Thought-provoking **unit questions** engage students with the topic and provide a **critical thinking framework** for the unit.

 Having the learning outcome is important because it gives students and teachers a clear idea of what the point of each task/activity in the unit is.
Lawrence Lawson, Palomar College, California

The Best Medicine Is Laughter

Reasons to Laugh

1   Laughter is good exercise. It makes you **breathe** quickly. Laughter makes your heart **rate** go up, and it can turn your face red. Laughter can even make you **cry**! Ten to fifteen minutes of laughing burns 50 calories[1]. It exercises your whole body.

2   Laughter has a positive **effect** on your health. It reduces high blood pressure[2] and can **prevent** some illnesses. Also,

 WHAT DO YOU THINK?

A. Complete the activities in a group.

1. What happens to you when you laugh for a long time? How do you feel after you laugh? Use ideas from the box or your own ideas.

breathe deeply	cry	heart rate increases
breathe quickly	face turns red	stomach hurts

B. Think about both Reading 1 and Reading 2 as you discuss the questions.

1. How can you get more laughter into your life?

2. Is it important for a person to have a sense of humor? Why or why not?

 One of the best features is your focus on developing materials of a high "interest level."
Troy Hammond, Tokyo Gakugei University, International Secondary School, Japan

Explicit skills instruction prepares students for academic success.

LANGUAGE SKILLS

Explicit instruction and practice in reading, vocabulary, grammar, and writing skills **help students achieve language proficiency.**

LEARNING OUTCOMES

Practice activities allow students to **master the skills** before they are evaluated at the end of the unit.

 WHAT DO YOU THINK?

Ask and answer the questions with a partner. Then choose one question and write two to three sentences about it in your notebook.

1. Ask and answer the questions in the chart. Check (✓) your partner's answers. Add one more question to the chart.

Do you laugh . . .	Never	Sometimes	Often
1. . . . when you are nervous?	☐	☐	☐
2. . . . when you hear a joke?	☐	☐	☐
3. . . . when you hear other people laugh?	☐	☐	☐
4. . . . when you are embarrassed?	☐	☐	☐
5. . . . when something surprises you?	☐	☐	☐
6. . . . when _____?	☐	☐	☐

2. Who are you with when you laugh a lot? Where are you? What are you doing?

Reading Skill   Identifying the topic sentence in a paragraph

The **topic sentence** explains the main idea of a paragraph. Other sentences in a paragraph support the topic sentence. Often, the topic sentence is the first sentence of a paragraph, but sometimes it is the second or third sentence. Finding the topic sentence helps you quickly understand what the paragraph is about.

> Robert Provine studied people and laughter. **He discovered that people laugh when they want to be friendly.** He watched people in the city walking and shopping. He found that 80 to 90 percent of laughter came after sentences like *I know* or *I'll see you later*. People didn't laugh because someone said something funny. People laughed because they wanted to be friendly with each other.

WRITING

Grammar   Sentences with *when*

You can combine two sentences with *when*. *When* introduces a situation or state, and it means that anytime that situation or state happens, something else happens.

- There is a comma if the sentence begins with *when*. There is no comma if *when* is in the middle of the sentence.
- When the subject in both sentences is the same, use a pronoun in the second part of the sentence.

They are nervous. → They laugh.
When they are nervous, they laugh.
They laugh **when** they are nervous.

Bob laughs. → He feels less stress.
When Bob laughs, he feels less stress.
Bob feels less stress **when** he laughs.

A. Write two sentences with *when*. Remember that *when* introduces the situation or state that causes another situation or state.

1. I go out with my friends. → I laugh a lot.
   a. _When I go out with my friends, I laugh a lot._
   b. _I laugh a lot when I go out with my friends._
2. You laugh. → Your blood pressure goes down.
   a. _____
   b. _____
3. He sees something funny. → He laughs.
   a. _____
   b. _____
4. You laugh. → You use calories.
   a. _____
   b. _____

 The tasks are simple, accessible, user-friendly, and very useful.
Jessica March, American University of Sharjah, U.A.E.

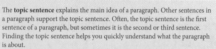

Vocabulary Skill Using the dictionary

When you see a word you don't know in a text, it helps to **identify the part of speech** of the word. *Nouns, verbs, adjectives,* and *adverbs* are examples of parts of speech. Knowing the part of speech helps you better understand the meaning and use of the word. If you aren't sure, you can find the part of speech for the vocabulary words in this book on the last page of each unit (in *Track Your Success*). You can also find the part of speech in a dictionary.

laugh¹ /læf/ *verb* (laughs, laugh·ing, laughed)
to make sounds to show that you are happy or that you think something is funny: *His jokes always make me laugh.*

laugh² /læf/ *noun* [*count*]
the sound you make when you are happy or when you think something is funny: *My brother has a loud laugh.* • *She told us a joke and we all had a good laugh* (= laughed a lot).

All dictionary entries are taken from the *Oxford American Dictionary for learners of English*.

LANGUAGE SKILLS

A **research-based vocabulary program** focuses students on the words they need to know academically and professionally, using skill strategies based on the same research as the Oxford dictionaries.

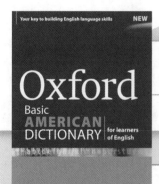

All dictionary entries are taken from the *Oxford American Dictionary for learners of English*.

The *Oxford Basic American Dictionary for learners of English* was designed with English learners in mind, and provides extra learning tools for pronunciation, verb types, basic grammar structures, and more.

The Oxford 2000 Keywords

The Oxford 2000 keywords encompasses the 2000 most important words to learn in English. It is based on a comprehensive analysis of the Oxford English Corpus, a two-billion word collection of English text, and on extensive research with both language and pedagogical experts.

The Academic Word List AWL

The Academic Word List was created by Averil Coxhead and contains **570 words that are commonly used in academic English**, such as in textbooks or articles across a wide range of academic subject areas. These words are a great place to start if you are studying English for academic purposes.

Clear learning outcomes focus students on the goals of instruction.

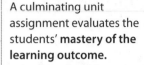

LEARNING OUTCOMES

A culminating unit assignment evaluates the students' **mastery of the learning outcome.**

Unit Assignment   Write a paragraph about what makes someone laugh

Q In this assignment, you are going to write a paragraph explaining what makes you or someone you know laugh. As you prepare your paragraph, think about the Unit Question, "What makes you laugh?" and refer to the Self-Assessment checklist on page 118.

For alternative unit assignments, see the *Q: Skills for Success Teacher's Handbook*.

PLAN AND WRITE

A. **BRAINSTORM** Think of situations that make you or someone you know laugh. Complete the chart with three situations for each type of laughter. Use vocabulary from the unit when you can.

Type of Laughter	Situations That Make You or Someone You Know Laugh
Nervous or embarrassed	1. 2. 3.
Something is funny	1. 2. 3.
Want to be friendly	1. 2. 3.

LEARNER CENTERED

Track Your Success allows students to **assess their own progress** and provides guidance on remediation.

Check (✓) the skills you learned. If you need more work on a skill, refer to the page(s) in parentheses.

READING	I can identify the topic sentence in a paragraph. (p. 106)
VOCABULARY	I can identify parts of speech in the dictionary. (p. 111)
GRAMMAR	I can recognize and use sentences with *when*. (p. 113)
WRITING	I can write a topic sentence. (p. 114)
LEARNING OUTCOME	I can explain what makes me or someone I know laugh.

 Students can check their learning . . . and they can focus on the essential points when they study.

Suh Yoomi, Seoul, South Korea

Q Online Practice

For the student
- **Easy-to-use:** a simple interface allows students to focus on enhancing their reading and writing skills, not learning a new software program
- **Flexible:** for use anywhere there's an Internet connection
- **Access code card:** a *Q Online Practice* access code is included with the student book. Use the access code to register for *Q Online Practice* at www.Qonlinepractice.com

For the teacher
- **Simple yet powerful:** automatically grades student exercises and tracks progress
- **Straightforward:** online management system to review, print, or export reports
- **Flexible:** for use in the classroom or easily assigned as homework
- **Access code card:** contact your sales rep for your *Q Online Practice* teacher's access code

Teacher Resources

Q Teacher's Handbook gives strategic support through:
- specific teaching notes for each activity
- ideas for ensuring student participation
- multilevel strategies and expansion activities
- the answer key
- special sections on 21st Century Skills and critical thinking
- a **Testing Program CD-ROM** with a customizable test for each unit

Oxford **Teachers' Club**

For additional resources visit the
Q: Skills for Success companion website at
www.oup.com/elt/teacher/Qskillsforsuccess

Q Class Audio includes:
- reading texts
- *The Q Classroom*

> It's an interesting, engaging series which provides plenty of materials that are easy to use in class, as well as instructionally promising.
>
> *Donald Weasenforth, Collin College, Texas*

UNIT	READING	WRITING
1 Names **Q How did you get your name?** **READING 1: Naming Around the World** A Magazine Article (Names) **READING 2: Naming the Blackberry** An Online Article (Marketing)	• Preview text • Read for main ideas • Read for details • Use glosses and footnotes to aid comprehension • Read and recognize different text types • Use charts to aid comprehension of text • Scan text to locate specific information	• Plan before writing • Revise, edit, and rewrite • Give feedback to peers and self-assess • Identify and capitalize proper nouns to improve accuracy in writing • Write well-formed, complete sentences using unit vocabulary and simple present tense
2 Work **Q What is a good job?** **READING 1: The Right Job for You** A Web Page (Jobs and Careers) **READING 2: The World of Work** A Magazine Article (Business)	• Preview text • Read for main ideas • Read for details • Use glosses and footnotes to aid comprehension • Read and recognize different text types • Use photos/pictures to activate schema before reading • Read titles and headings to prepare to read • Complete a survey to relate topic to self	• Plan before writing • Revise, edit, and rewrite • Give feedback to peers and self-assess • Recognize differences between fragments and complete sentences • Write complete sentences about the unit topic
3 Long Distance **Q Why do people immigrate to other countries?** **READING 1: The World in a City** A Web Page (Immigration) **READING 2: Immigrant Stories** A Magazine Article (Sociology)	• Preview text • Read for main ideas • Read for details • Use glosses and footnotes to aid comprehension • Read and recognize different text types • Skim for main ideas to aid comprehension of text • Anticipate reading content by analyzing text features such as headings, pictures, and captions • Read maps to locate selected information	• Plan before writing • Revise, edit, and rewrite • Give feedback to peers and self-assess • Use conjunctions *and* and *but* to connect simple sentences • Write sentences about the unit topic
4 Positive Thinking **Q What are the benefits of positive thinking?** **READING 1: The Power of Positive Thinking?** A Magazine Article (Psychology) **READING 2: The Lost Horse** An Old Chinese Story (Literature)	• Preview text • Read for main ideas • Read for details • Use glosses and footnotes to aid comprehension • Read and recognize different text types • Complete a quiz to gain background information on a topic • Make inferences to understand ideas not stated directly in the text	• Plan before writing • Revise, edit, and rewrite • Give feedback to peers and self-assess • Use time order words to show the sequence of events in writing • Write a story about the unit topic

VOCABULARY	GRAMMAR	CRITICAL THINKING	UNIT OUTCOME
• Match definitions • Define new terms • Understand meaning from context • Use the dictionary to locate correct word spellings using alphabetical order	• Simple present: Affirmative and negative statements	• Reflect on the unit question • Connect ideas across readings • Set and achieve goals • Apply unit tips and use *Q Online Practice* to become a strategic learner • Support answers with examples and opinions • Analyze reasons behind likes and dislikes • Apply information from reading to own situation	• Write about a name that you like, giving information about the name.
• Match definitions • Define new terms • Understand meaning from context • Expand vocabulary through recognizing nouns and verbs with same forms	• Verbs + infinitives: *like, want, need*	• Reflect on the unit question • Connect ideas across readings • Set and achieve goals • Apply unit tips and use *Q Online Practice* to become a strategic learner • Apply information from reading to own situation • Support opinions with reasons	• Describe the duties of the job you want and give reasons that it is a good job for you.
• Match definitions • Define new terms • Understand meaning from context • Learn word roots to expand vocabulary	• *There* and *to be* in the simple present and simple past	• Reflect on the unit question • Connect ideas across readings • Set and achieve goals • Apply unit tips and use *Q Online Practice* to become a strategic learner • Support opinions with examples • Express likes and preferences • Apply information from reading to own situation	• Explain how a place changed because of international immigration or culture.
• Match definitions • Define new terms • Understand meaning from context • Use phrasal verbs to expand vocabulary	• Simple past with regular and irregular verbs	• Reflect on the unit question • Connect ideas across readings • Set and achieve goals • Apply unit tips and use *Q Online Practice* to become a strategic learner • Compare different ways of thinking about a topic • Apply information from reading to own situation	• Write about a time when you or someone you know changed a situation with positive thinking.

UNIT	READING	WRITING
5 Vacation ⍰ **Why is vacation important?** **READING 1:** Vacation from Work An Email (Vacation) **READING 2:** Vacation from School Letters to the Editor (Opinion)	• Preview text • Read for main ideas • Read for details • Use glosses and footnotes to aid comprehension • Read and recognize different text types • Use photos/pictures to activate schema before reading • Read charts, graphs, and tables to organize and interpret information and statistics • Compare information in readings to see similarities and differences	• Plan before writing • Revise, edit, and rewrite • Write paragraphs of different genres • Give feedback to peers and self-assess • Use topic sentences, supporting sentences, and concluding sentences to write a well formed paragraph • Write a paragraph giving reasons
6 Laughter ⍰ **What makes you laugh?** **READING 1:** What Is Laughter? A News Magazine Article (Laughter) **READING 2:** The Best Medicine Is Laughter A Website Article (Health)	• Preview text • Read for main ideas • Read for details • Use glosses and footnotes to aid comprehension • Read and recognize different text types • Use photos/pictures to activate schema before reading • Identify topic sentences to aid comprehension of text	• Plan before writing • Revise, edit, and rewrite • Write paragraphs of different genres • Give feedback to peers and self-assess • Construct a good topic sentence to make ideas clear when writing • Write a paragraph of explanation
7 Music ⍰ **How does music make you feel?** **READING 1:** Music and Shopping A Textbook Excerpt (Marketing) **READING 2:** Music and the Movies A Website Article (The Arts)	• Preview text • Read for main ideas • Read for details • Use glosses and footnotes to aid comprehension • Read and recognize different text types • Use photos/pictures to activate schema before reading • Identify supporting sentences and details to aid comprehension of text	• Plan before writing • Revise, edit, and rewrite • Write paragraphs of different genres • Give feedback to peers and self-assess • Write supporting sentences and details to support topic sentences • Write a paragraph about feelings

VOCABULARY	GRAMMAR	CRITICAL THINKING	UNIT OUTCOME
• Match definitions • Define new terms • Understand meaning from context • Identify compound nouns to expand vocabulary	• Conjunction: *because*	• Reflect on the unit question • Connect ideas across readings • Set and achieve goals • Apply unit tips and use *Q Online Practice* to become a strategic learner • Apply information from reading to own situation • Identify reasons for/against a position • Use a chart to organize information	• Write a paragraph explaining how much vacation time you need.
• Match definitions • Define new terms • Understand meaning from context • Use the dictionary to learn parts of speech	• Sentences with *when*	• Reflect on the unit question • Connect ideas across readings • Set and achieve goals • Apply unit tips and use *Q Online Practice* to become a strategic learner • Apply information from reading to own situation • Identify reasons for/against a position	• Explain what makes you or someone you know laugh.
• Match definitions • Define new terms • Understand meaning from context • Build vocabulary using prefixes: *un-*	• Prepositions of location	• Reflect on the unit question • Connect ideas across readings • Set and achieve goals • Apply unit tips and use *Q Online Practice* to become a strategic learner • Express likes and preferences • Apply ideas from reading to different situations	• Identify what type of music you like, where you listen to it, and how it makes you feel.

UNIT	READING	WRITING
8 Honesty **Q** **Is it ever OK to lie?** **READING 1: The Lies People Tell** A Magazine Article (Honesty) **READING 2: Honesty and Parenting** Internet Chat Room Postings (Parenting)	• Preview text • Read for main ideas • Read for details • Use glosses and footnotes to aid comprehension • Read and recognize different text types • Match pronouns with their referents to see text cohesion • Make inferences to deepen comprehension of text • Skim text before reading to get the main idea	• Plan before writing • Revise, edit, and rewrite • Write paragraphs of different genres • Give feedback to peers and self-assess • Write concluding sentences to close a paragraph • Write an opinion paragraph
9 Life Changes **Q** **How are children and adults different?** **READING 1: What Is An Adult?** An Excerpt from a Textbook (Life Changes) **READING 2: Becoming an Adult** Magazine Blog Postings (Anthropology)	• Preview text • Read for main ideas • Read for details • Use glosses and footnotes to aid comprehension • Read and recognize different text types • Mark the margins to engage actively with the text • Skim text before reading to get the main idea • Use charts to organize information from reading	• Plan before writing • Revise, edit, and rewrite • Write paragraphs of different genres • Give feedback to peers and self-assess • Construct a timeline to sequence events in a story • Write a narrative paragraph
10 Fear **Q** **What are you afraid of?** **READING 1: A Dangerous World?** A Magazine Article (Fear) **READING 2: Can We Trust Our Fears?** An Online Article (Psychology)	• Preview text • Read for main ideas • Read for details • Use glosses and footnotes to aid comprehension • Read and recognize different text types • Use photos/pictures to activate schema before reading • Distinguish fact from opinion to read critically • Scan text to locate facts and opinions	• Plan before writing • Revise, edit, and rewrite • Write paragraphs of different genres • Give feedback to peers and self-assess • Use the transitional expression *however* to contrast ideas in writing • Use correct punctuation with *however* • Write a paragraph of explanation

VOCABULARY	GRAMMAR	CRITICAL THINKING	UNIT OUTCOME
• Match definitions • Define new terms • Understand meaning from context • Learn collocations to expand vocabulary	• Infinitives of purpose: *in order* + infinitive	• Reflect on the unit question • Connect ideas across readings • Set and achieve goals • Apply unit tips and use *Q Online Practice* to become a strategic learner • Express opinions • agreement/disagreement • Use a T-chart to organize information	• Write a paragraph that explains your opinion about whether or not it is OK to lie in an online forum.
• Match definitions • Define new terms • Understand meaning from context • Use the dictionary to identify different definitions of the same word	• Clauses with *after* and *after that*	• Reflect on the unit question • Connect ideas across readings • Set and achieve goals • Apply unit tips and use *Q Online Practice* to become a strategic learner • Apply information from reading to own situation • Identify reasons for/ against a position	• Describe events in your life that made you feel like an adult.
• Match definitions • Define new terms • Understand meaning from context • Recognize word families to expand vocabulary	• Comparative adjectives	• Reflect on the unit question • Connect ideas across readings • Set and achieve goals • Apply unit tips and use *Q Online Practice* to become a strategic learner • Justify opinions with reasons	• Describe an unreasonable fear and explain how it can be avoided.

READING • scanning for information	**LEARNING OUTCOME**
VOCABULARY • using the dictionary	
WRITING • capitalizing proper nouns	Write about a name that you like, giving
GRAMMAR • simple present	information about the name.

▶ *Reading and Writing 1, page 3*

Preview the Unit

Learning Outcome

1. Ask for a volunteer to read the unit skills, then the unit learning outcome *(Write about a name that you like, giving information about the name).*

2. Explain: *This is what you are expected to be able to do by the unit's end. The learning outcome explains how you are going to be evaluated. With this outcome in mind, you should focus on learning these skills (Reading, Vocabulary, Writing, Grammar) that will support your goal of writing about a name that you like and giving information about that name. This can also help you act as mentors in the classroom to help the other students meet this outcome.*

A (10 minutes)

1. Elicit boys' names and girls' names and write them on the board. Ensure that names from various cultures are represented. Alternatively, have students write names on the board themselves.

2. Put students in pairs or small groups to discuss the first two questions.

3. Call on volunteers to share their ideas with the class. Ask questions: *Which names are popular these days?* Point out that some names can be both boys' and girls' names in English (e.g., Chris, Lee, Jordan). *Is it important to have a unique name? Why or why not?*

4. Focus students' attention on the photo. Have a volunteer describe the photo to the class.

5. Read the final question aloud. Ask three or four students to take turns reading the names. Ask remaining students to stand when they hear a name that's interesting. Tally number

of respondents. After they've finished, write the top two or three names on the board and ask volunteers to explain why those names are considered interesting.

Activity A Answers, p. 3
Answers will vary. Possible answers:
1. I like my name. I like the name Pablo.
   I like the name Pierre.
2. I like the name Sarah. I like the name Liliana.
3. Students' own answers.

B (10 minutes)

1. Introduce the Unit Question, *How did you get your name?* Ask related information questions or questions about personal experience to help students prepare for answering the Unit Question: *Who gave you your name? What does your name mean? Think of people in your family (brother, sister, or cousin, for example) who are named after/ for an older family member. Maybe they are named after your mom, dad, aunt, uncle, grandmother, or grandfather. Why were they named after that person?*

2. Put students in small groups and give each group a piece of poster paper and a marker.

3. Read the Unit Question aloud. Give students a minute to silently consider their answers to the question. Tell students to pass the paper and marker around the group. Direct each group member to write an answer to the question. Encourage them to help one another.

4. Ask each group to choose a reporter to read the answers to the class. Point out and elicit similarities and differences among the answers. Make a group list that incorporates the most common answers and post it.

Answers will vary. Possible answers: My mother gave me my name. My grandfather gave my parents the idea for my name. My name came from an old story from my country.

The Q Classroom (5 minutes)
🔊 CD1, Track 02

1. Play The Q Classroom. Use the example from the audio to help students continue the conversation. Ask: *How did the students answer the question?*

2. Marcus discusses a naming tradition in his family (that the oldest boy of a generation gets the same name: Marcus). Ask: *Do you have similar naming traditions in your family or in your culture? What other naming traditions do you have in your family?*

▶ *Reading and Writing 1, page 4*

C (10 minutes)

1. Have students look at the name on the ID card and ask if they notice a difference between the first letter of each name and the rest of the letters in the name. Remind students that the first letter of every name must be capitalized. Mention that *upper case* letters and *capital* letters are the same thing. Mention also that capitalization is formally presented in this Unit on page 16.

2. Model the capitalization rule by writing your name on the board in all lower case letters. Then ask students which letters need to be capitalized, and capitalize those letters. Then ask a volunteer to label your name with the terms *given name, middle name, family name,* and *full name,* using the ID card labeling in the exercise as a model.

3. Ask for another volunteer to come to the board and write his or her full name. Have students ask him/her questions 1–4, and have the volunteer point to and label his/her answer with the terms *given name, middle name, family name,* and *full name.*

4. Next, have students complete C with a partner. Circulate around the room and provide help and clarification as needed.

MULTILEVEL OPTION

Have lower-level students pair with higher-level students. Lower-level students can listen as the higher-level students interview each other and watch as they write their answers.

Then allow higher-level students to assist lower-level students as needed as they interview each other.

Tip for Success (1 minute)

1. Read the Tip for Success aloud.

2. Point out any differences between the name labels in English-speaking countries compared to students' home countries.

D (20 minutes)

1. Explain to students that they will introduce their partner to another pair of students. Once students have introduced their partners in the small group, they will introduce their partner to the class.

2. Model the introduction sequence by introducing one of the volunteers from Activity C to the class. *I'd like to introduce my partner. This is* [volunteer's full name]. Write introduction language on the board. Encourage the second speaker to say: *And I'd like to introduce my partner….*

3. Elicit prior knowledge from students about the contraction *I'd.* If no student knows, explain the contraction. Point out that conversations in many languages often include contractions. For example, *al hotel* contracts to *a el hotel* in Spanish (*to the hotel*).

4. Begin small group introductions with four to six students per group. Monitor the groups' progress and note issues that the whole class might benefit from hearing (e.g., *I like…* instead of *I'd like*).

5. Facilitate whole group introductions. Bring up issues that the whole class would benefit from hearing.

6. Review introductions by asking volunteers to stand up. Then, ask the class to say the standing student's name.

7. Choose two or three students and ask volunteers to ask them the Unit Question: *How did you get your name?*

EXPANSION ACTIVITY: Name Scramble (10 minutes)

1. Ask students to write their full names on slips of paper but have students jumble their given, middle, and family names. For example, *Juan Alfredo Gomez* might become *Alfredo Gomez Juan.*

2. Have students stand up and find a partner. Students will exchange slips of paper and take turns saying their partner's full names by asking: *What's my name?* Partners will look at the slip of paper and try to unscramble their partner's full name, and reply: *Your name is [full name.]* Once each partner's name is successfully unscrambled

(it may take several attempts), students will hold up their slip of paper, signaling that they are ready for a new partner.

3. Students will seek out other students with slips in the air and initiate the sequence again: A: *What is my name?* B: *Your name is [full name].*

4. If there is an uneven number of students in the classroom, you may participate as well.

READING

▶ *Reading and Writing 1, page 5*

READING 1:
Naming Around the World

VOCABULARY (10 minutes)

1. Write bolded vocabulary on the board and probe for prior knowledge. Ask: *What words do you already know? What do those words mean?* When writing nouns on board, use articles (*a, an, the*) when appropriate. When writing verbs, use the infinitive form. Using articles and infinitive forms can help students differentiate nouns and verbs, especially when the words are the same (e.g., *a sound* vs. *to sound*).

2. Put students in groups of two or three and have them complete the activity. Encourage students to make guesses and emphasize that it's OK to be wrong.

3. Ask different volunteers to read sentences 1–8 in turn. Ask the class if they are reading a noun, a verb, or an adjective. Correct as needed.

4. Provide or elicit correct answers.

MULTILEVEL OPTION

Group lower-level students and assist them with the task. Provide alternate example sentences to help them understand the words. Here are some example sentences for possibly tricky vocabulary:

*As a mother, there is one **generation** above me (my parents) and one below me (my children). It's a **tradition** in my family to take a trip together every summer. Birds in spring make beautiful **sounds**. Cereal is a **popular** breakfast food in the United States.*

Have higher-level students complete the activity individually and then compare answers with a partner. Ask the pairs to write an additional sample sentence for each vocabulary item. Have volunteers write one of their sentences on the board. Correct the sentences with the whole class, focusing on the use of the given vocabulary item rather than other grammatical issues.

Vocabulary Answers, p. 5
a. relatives;   **b.** generation;   **c.** choose;   **d.** sound;
e. tradition;   **f.** popular;   **g.** poem;   **h.** create

 For additional practice with the vocabulary, have students visit *Q Online Practice*.

▶ *Reading and Writing 1, page 6*

PREVIEW READING 1 (15 minutes)

1. Write the title of the article on the board (*Naming Around the World*). Have students brainstorm what they think they will learn from the article.

2. Next, ask students to brainstorm names of different groups of people living in the world (e.g., Thai, Tongan, Ukrainian, Guatemalan). Write ideas on the board. Point out that the name of each group is capitalized—just like people's names.

3. Ask students what they know about how names are given in the cultures listed on the board.

4. Have a student volunteer read the directions for Preview Reading 1 aloud. Point out that another way to say *look quickly* is *scan*. Encourage students to scan the text for the three answers. Elicit the answers.

5. Tell students they should review their answers after reading as their answers may change after reading the article.

Preview Reading 1 Answer, p. 6
1. Chinese;   **2.** African-American;   **3.** Spanish

Reading 1 Background Note

While naming traditions in some countries might buck historic practice (and thereby create new traditions), naming traditions in other countries might be diametrically opposed to what people in other cultures see as traditional naming practices.

In the United States and other countries such as Canada, England, and Australia, instead of wives taking husbands' names as their own, families sometimes choose hyphenated names (e.g., Sawyer-Hutchins) or husbands and wives keep their own family names. Less often, one can also find hybrid names (e.g., Wang and Berkman become Wangman), or new family names altogether (e.g., Ecklund and Edwards becoming Holman). New family traditions and ways of naming change often.

In Latin American countries, it is traditional for children to take both parents' family names—in addition to children's first and middle names. The first family name is the father's (and is the official family name); the second is the mother's. Upon marriage, a woman won't drop her family names, and might also adopt her husband's family name. Thus, some women might have a full name that consists of a first name, a middle name, and several family names!

READ

 CD1, Track 03

1. Instruct students to read the article *Naming Around the World*.

2. Play the audio and have students follow along.

▶ *Reading and Writing 1, page 8*

MAIN IDEAS (10 minutes)

1. Preview the statements with students and ensure they understand the vocabulary—including the difference between true and false. Point out the title of the activity and the fact that this activity will always practice finding the main ideas of a reading.

2. Go over the sample answer. Ask students to read and complete the activity on their own.

3. Read the statements. Have students raise their left hands for false and their right hands for true. Provide or confirm correct answers. Check for understanding.

Main Idea Answers, p. 8
1. F; **2.** T; **3.** T; **4.** F

DETAILS (15 minutes)

1. Direct students to read the statements and complete the activity.

2. Have students compare answers with a partner.

3. Direct the students to look back at the article to check their answers.

4. Go over the answers with the class.

Details Answers, p. 8
1. African-American; **2.** Chinese; **3.** Spanish;
4. Chinese; **5.** Chinese; **6.** Spanish;
7. African-American

For additional practice with reading comprehension, have students visit *Q Online Practice*.

Critical Thinking Tip (1 minute)

1. Read the tip aloud.

2. Point out to students that identifying is not only a good way to show that you have learned the material but also a good way to pinpoint things you may already know in new material.

Critical Q: Expansion Activity

Identify

1. Put students in groups and have them think of items/brands they couldn't live life without.

2. Tell the students to develop a list of reasons why those items/brands are so important.

3. Direct students to think of their grandparents' generation. Ask: *How did they live without these items/brands? What were their lives like? Were their lives worse?*

4. Discuss as a class: *How has advertising caused people to think that items/brands are something we need instead of something we want? How have advertising traditions changed over the past few generations? Is such advertising good or bad? Why?*

Reading Skill:
Scanning for information (20 minutes)

1. Have students brainstorm different kinds of texts (e.g., newspaper articles, weather reports, phone books). Elicit types of information students might find by scanning these text types. Bring in some examples, if possible. (Bring in realia such as train tickets and brochures if available.)

2. Present the scanning explanation. Answer any questions.

3. Put the Unit Question *How did you get your name?* on the board. Ask students what the important words to underline are. For example, *How did you get your name?*

4. Elicit/provide a few more questions for students to use as practice for underlining important words, for example, *Where is the bus stop? Why are you going to school every day?*

5. Check comprehension by asking questions: *What makes these words "important"? Are nouns important words? Are verbs? What kinds of words are not "important" words?*

▶ *Reading and Writing 1, page 9*

A (10 minutes)

1. Focus students' attention on the underlined words.
2. Have them find the answers by scanning the article. Remind them to circle their answers.
3. Check answers as a class.

> **Reading Skill A Answers, p. 9**
> **1-1.** the given/first name;
> **1-2.** the father's family/last name;
> **1-3.** the mother's family/last name;
> **2.** Answers will vary but may include: Denzel, Kavonte, etc.

B (15 minutes)

1. Direct students to underline important words in each question. For example, in sentence number one, underline: *What are two Chinese relatives with the same generation name?*
2. Ask students to find answers by scanning the article. Have students take a close look at the article's charts to help find the answers.
3. Check answers as a class.

> **Reading Skill B Answers, p. 9**
> Possible answers:
> **1.** Li, Bei, and Jun.
> **2.** Katisha and Wanika.
> **3.** Chavez and Hernandez.

 For additional practice with scanning for information, have students visit *Q Online Practice*.

Skill Note

In language, there are *content words* and *structure words*. When speaking, *content words* are often the words that are emphasized (e.g., nouns, verbs, adjectives). They provide the main content, so these are the words that speakers want their listeners to focus on. *Structure words* are often the words, like prepositions and articles, that link utterances together. Typically in spoken language, *structure words* are unstressed and sometimes incomprehensible to language learners.

When scanning for and underlining "important words," students are typically underlining the *content words* found in spoken language. Such practice can translate into helping students know which words to emphasize when they speak.

1. Ask students to read the statements and reflect on their answers, making checks for *Yes* or *No*.
2. Seat students in small groups and assign roles: a group leader to make sure everyone contributes, a note-taker to record the group's ideas, a reporter to share the group's ideas with the class, and a timekeeper to watch the clock.
3. Give students five minutes to discuss the statements. Call time if conversations are winding down. Allow extra time if necessary.
4. Call on each group's reporter to share ideas with the class.
5. Have each student choose one of the statements they answered *yes* to and write 2–3 sentences explaining why the answer was *yes*.
6. Call on volunteers to share ideas with the class.

> **MULTILEVEL OPTION**
>
> In groups with lower-level students, have higher-level students write one or two more statements that might be used in this activity (e.g., *We wait until after the child is born to create a name*). Have lower-level students respond to these statements with a *Yes* or a *No*.

> **What Do You Think? Answers, p. 9**
> Answers will vary.

Learning Outcome

Use the learning outcome to frame the purpose and relevance of Reading 1. Ask: *What did you learn from Reading 1 that prepares you to write about a name that you like, giving information about the name?*

▶ *Reading and Writing 1, page 10*

READING 2:
Naming the BlackBerry

VOCABULARY (15 minutes)

1. Write the seven vocabulary words in a list on the board two or three times, leaving some space between the lists. Each list should contain the seven bolded vocabulary words.
2. Divide the class into as many groups as there are lists on the board and line groups up an equal distance from the board, in front of one of the word lists.

3. Read one of the definitions. When you do, the first student in line from each group should run up to the board and "slap" the word to which the definition refers. Correct as necessary. Each "runner" rewrites any words that have been erased from being "slapped" and goes to the back of his or her group's line.

4. Repeat until students "slap" correct words most of the time.

5. Give students time to complete the vocabulary activity in the book.

> **Vocabulary Answers, p. 10**
> **a.** electronics;   **b.** connect;   **c.** similar;
> **d.** attention;   **e.** describe;   **f.** company;
> **g.** product

 For additional practice with the vocabulary, have students visit *Q Online Practice*.

MULTILEVEL OPTION

Have lower-level students rewrite the words that are "slapped" off the board.

Have higher-level students provide an example sentence with the vocabulary item they "slap."

▶ *Reading and Writing 1, page 11*
PREVIEW READING 2   (5 minutes)

1. Ask students: *What is a blackberry? What is a BlackBerry®?* Have students pair up and complete the Preview Reading 2 activity.

2. Before reading the article, ask students: *What skill have we learned that will help you read this article quickly?* (Scanning). *How can it help?*

3. Tell students they should review their answer for Preview Reading 2 after reading.

Reading 2 Background Note

Not all "brandings" are as successful as BlackBerry®. Take the case of this car brand: the Chevy Nova. In the United States, Chevrolet's marketing campaign for the Nova was highly successful. They sold many Novas; customers were happy. However, when the company extended its campaign into Latin America, the story goes that the Chevrolet met with unexpected results. The Chevy Nova, in English, commanded a sense of strength. In Spanish, *Nova* was too similar to the Spanish *no va*, meaning "it doesn't go." Who would buy a car that doesn't go?

 CD1, Track 04

1. Instruct students to read the article *Naming the BlackBerry®*.

2. Play the audio and have students follow along.

▶ *Reading and Writing 1, page 12*
MAIN IDEAS   (5 minutes)

1. Preview the statements with students and ensure they understand the vocabulary—including the difference between true and false.

2. Ask students to read and complete the activity individually.

3. Read the statements. Have students raise their left hands for false and their right hands for true. Provide or confirm correct answers.

> **Main Idea Answers, p. 12**
> **1.** F;   **2.** T;   **3.** F;   **4.** T

Tip for Success   (1 minute)

1. Read the Tip for Success on page 12.

2. Remind students that purposeful *re*reading is a key part of reading.

DETAILS   (10 minutes)

1. Direct students to read the question (*Why is BlackBerry® a good name?*), read the eight statements, and complete the activity.

2. Have students compare answers with a partner.

3. Direct the students to look back at the article to check their answers.

4. Go over the answers with the class.

> **Details Answers, pp. 12–13**
> 1, 3, 5, 6, and 7.

 For additional practice with reading comprehension, have students visit *Q Online Practice*.

▶ *Reading and Writing 1, page 13*
WHAT DO YOU THINK?

A   (10 minutes)

1. Ask students to read Activity A and fill in the chart, working in a group.

2. Share answers in small groups and discuss this question: *Do you like these brand names? Why or why not?* Ask students to use vocabulary from Activity A, Part 2 to supplement their answers.

3. Ask students to complete Activity A, Part 3 individually. Ask students to share their sentences with a partner. Choose volunteers to share sentences with class.

> **Activity A Answers, p. 13**
> **1.** and **2.** Answers will vary;
> **3.** Answers will vary. Possible answers: I like the name BlackBerry®. It is easy to say. I don't like the name Zyrtec. It doesn't have a nice sound.

Tip for Success (1 minute)

Read the tip. Remind students that there are many words in English that can be both nouns and verbs (e.g., *train, sleep, drive*).

B (15 minutes)

1. Tell the students that they should think about both Reading 1 and Reading 2 as they answer these questions with a partner. Students will choose one of the questions and write 2–3 sentences in response. This can be done as homework.

2. Ask students to read their sentences with a partner.

3. Call on each pair to share ideas with the class.

Learning Outcome

Use the learning outcome to frame the purpose and relevance of Readings 1 and 2 and the Critical Q activity. Ask: *What did you learn from Reading 2 that prepares you to write about a name that you like, giving information about the name?*

▶ *Reading and Writng 1, page 14*

Vocabulary Skill: Using the dictionary (15 minutes)

1. Ask students: *How many of you use a dictionary? Why do you use a dictionary?* Explain to students why you think dictionaries are important for language learners (e.g., *helps students discover parts of speech; provides collocation patterns; provides pronunciation guidelines*).

2. Explain that dictionaries organize words in alphabetical order. Write three vocabulary words from Readings 1 and 2 on the board in alphabetical order (e.g., *electronics, poem,* and *similar*). Review rules for second and third letters

(page 14 of the *Student Text*).

3. Check comprehension. Write three more vocabulary words on the board (e.g., *popular, sound,* and *product*) and ask students to place in alphabetical order. Ask students: *Which letter do we look at first when placing words in alphabetical order? What if the first letter is the same? How do we order words based upon their second letters?*

Skill Note

Dictionaries are a valuable tool for language learners; they are a window through which they can understand messages. Sometimes, however, dictionaries are unable to provide a context for new vocabulary words. In those cases, students may look up a word and then forget its meaning before the next class meeting. Help students make an extra effort to retain new vocabulary found in dictionaries by asking students to maintain their own personal dictionaries.

For each entry, which could be organized by date, students could have three columns: (1) the word, (2) the definition, and (3) the sentence the word was found in—or a unique sentence that they write. Set aside a few minutes of class, at the beginning or the end, for students to review their growing list of entries. Take these personalized dictionaries home periodically and organize tasks around their "found" vocabulary items.

A (5 minutes)

1. Have students work individually to complete the activity. Make sure there are enough dictionaries for everyone. Once complete, place students with partners to compare answers.

2. Go over the answers with the class. Elicit example sentences for some of the vocabulary items.

> **Activity A Answers, p. 14**
> Answers will vary.

▶ *Reading and Writing 1, page 15*

B (10 minutes)

1. Write the four words from each item on individual pieces of large white paper. Have four students at a time go to the front of the class and hold the paper so that the class can read the words for that item but they cannot.

2. Have students in the "audience" alphabetize the words by telling the students where to move (e.g., *Neda, move to the left of Sergio. Phan, stand next to*

Neda). Ask students to write their answers in their books. Switch students for each item.

Activity B Answers, p. 15
1. baby, parent, tradition, world;
2. name, next, not, number;
3. family, famous, fast, father;
4. after, also, and, any;
5. can, child, children, choose;
6. the, their, then, there

 For additional practice with using the dictionary, have students visit *Q Online Practice.*

▶ *Reading and Writing 1, page 16*

WRITING

Writing Skill: Capitalizing proper nouns (15 minutes)

1. Remind students about the capitalization activity you did with the ID Card on page 4. Ask: *Which letters had to be capitalized?* Select a few students to write their full names on the board. Underline capital letters. Remind students: *Names have to be capitalized. Why?* Have students find the answer in the presentation text on proper nouns.

2. Go over the information in this presentation.

3. Check comprehension by asking questions: *What are some examples of proper nouns that you've seen in the textbook so far? Can you think of more examples? What are examples of common nouns that you've seen in the textbook so far? What commons nouns can you see in this classroom? Which nouns in this classroom have names that need to be capitalized?*

A (5 minutes)

1. Direct students to read the directions for the activity before reading the text. Remind students that proper nouns can consist of more than one word (like someone's name). Have them find all of the examples of capitalized proper nouns in the text (e.g., *Chicago River*).

2. Ask students to read the text and underline the seven proper nouns.

3. Go over the answers with the class.

Activity A Answers, p. 16
Chicago, Illinois, the United States of America, Native Americans, Algonquins, Chicago River, Lake Michigan

▶ *Reading and Writing 1, page 17*

B (10 minutes)

1. Direct students to complete the activity individually, checking their answers with a partner once done.

2. When done, have pairs consider the following question: *Why is each word considered a proper noun?* Share opinions with the class. Answers may include: *a person's name, a place's name, a brand name,* etc.

Activity B Answers, p. 17
1. William;	2. Broadway;	3. Toshiba;
4. Subaru;	5. Friday;	6. Hard Rock Cafe;
7. November;	8. Paris;	9. Ms. Andrews;
10. Mount Everest		

C (10 minutes)

1. Direct students to complete the activity individually, checking their answers with a partner once done.

2. Go over answers with the class. Discuss why each word is considered a proper noun.

Activity C Answers, p. 17
Celedonio, Spanish, Latin, Celedonio, Romero, Malaga, Spain

 For additional practice with capitalizing proper nouns, have students visit *Q Online Practice.*

▶ *Reading and Writing 1, page 18*

Grammar: Simple present (15 minutes)

1. Go over the information in this presentation.

2. Check comprehension of the grammar presentation by asking questions and eliciting/providing examples of each: *In what three ways do we often use the simple present? Who can give me an example of a sentence in simple present? Who can give me an example of a negative sentence with have? How do you conjugate* I am*? What two words are in the contraction* aren't*? Which pronouns require an* s *at the end of the verb?*

3. Write three infinitive verbs on the board (e.g., *to like, to eat,* and *to see*) and conjugate them together for affirmative and negative.

4. Write *to be* on the board and have students conjugate the simple present for each pronoun. Have students describe their partners, using simple present conjugations of *to be* (e.g., *She is tall. They are nice.*).

5. Practice present tense recognition. Ask students to reread Reading 1 or Reading 2 and underline the present tense verbs they find.

6. Review contractions (e.g., *I'm, she's, we're*).

Skill Note

Verb endings carry a lot of information. Often, verb endings are the cues that listeners use to piece together meaning—including contractions. Ensure that students clearly articulate the ending sounds of present simple verbs and contractions. Have students practice by first writing a list of five conjugated verbs from the grammar section (e.g., *I'm, has, he's, does,* and *they're*). Put students in pairs and have each student give their partner a dictation from their lists. When the pair has completed their dictations, have students compare the speaker's list to the writer's list to see if the speaker articulated, or the writer heard, the proper endings. Explain: *The best way to be able to hear these endings is to first be able to say them.*

▶ *Reading and Writing 1, page 19*

A (5 minutes)

1. Direct students to circle the correct verb form.

2. Put students in pairs to discuss their answers.

3. Call on volunteers to share their ideas with the class.

> **Activity A Answers, p. 19**
> **1.** are; **2.** have; **3.** give; **4.** gets;
> **5.** gives; **6.** mean; **7.** means

▶ *Reading and Writing 1, page 20*

B (10 minutes)

1. Direct students to complete the sentences.

2. Put students in pairs to discuss their answers.

3. Choose volunteers to write answers on the board.

> **Activity B Answers, p. 20**
> **1.** are; **2.** have; **3.** doesn't name; **4.** cook;
> **5.** has; **6.** says; **7.** tells; **8.** gives

 For additional practice with the simple present tense, have students visit *Q Online Practice*.

Tip for Success (1 minute)

1. Read the tip aloud.

2. Point out that only *he/she/it* conjugations include an *s* at the end of the present tense verb—even with the auxiliary verb *does*. Elicit and provide examples of this point. (e.g., *He eats; It rains* everyday.)

Q Unit Assignment:
Write sentences about a name you like

Unit Question (5 minutes)

Refer students back to the ideas they discussed at the beginning of the unit about how people get their names and why people like certain names (people names and brand names). Cue students if necessary by asking specific questions about the content of the unit: *What kind of naming traditions did we talk about? What did our readings tell us about the importance of names?* Read the direction lines for the assignment together to ensure understanding.

Learning Outcome

1. Tie the Unit Assignment to the unit learning outcome. Say: *The outcome for this unit is to write about a name that you like, giving information about the name. This Unit Assignment is going to let you practice your writing and editing skills by writing a few sentences about a name that you like. Explaining why you like something is a skill that you will use many times in your academic and professional career.*

2. Explain that you are going to use a rubric similar to their Self-Assessment checklist on p. 22 to grade their Unit Assignments. You can also share a copy of the Unit Assignment Rubric (on p. 12 of this *Teacher's Handbook*) with the students.

Plan and Write

Brainstorm

A (10 minutes)

1. Direct students to complete Activity A with a partner and share answers with another pair.

▶ *Reading and Writing 1, page 21*

Plan

B (10 minutes)

1. Have students answer the questions with the same partner. Ask them to provide extended answers (more than one word) so that they can come up with language they can use in their writings. Encourage students to use words like *because* to extend their answers.

2. Circulate around the room, providing help and answering questions as needed.

Write

C (20 minutes)

1. Go over the directions and example.

2. Remind students to use vocabulary items from the unit where possible and the simple present tense. Review the vocabulary and the simple present if you feel students need a review.

3. If appropriate, give students a specific number and/or a list of vocabulary items they must use.

Alternative Unit Assignments

Assign or have students choose one of these assignments to do instead of, or in addition to, the Unit Assignment.

1. Choose one family member's name that you like. Write several sentences about why you like the name.

2. Draw your family tree. Use the family tree on page 7 to help you.

3. Work in a small group. Think of an idea for a new sports drink. What does it taste like? Make a good name for the drink. Explain your reasons why the name is a good one.

 For an additional unit assignment, have students visit *Q Online Practice*.

▶ *Reading and Writing 1, page 22*

Revise and Edit

Peer Review

A (15–20 minutes)

1. Pair students and direct them to read each other's work.

2. Ask students to answer the questions and discuss them.

3. Give students suggestions of helpful feedback: *I liked your writing because…. Can you be clearer about why you like the name? I think you can use more vocabulary words.*

Rewrite

B (15–20 minutes)

Students should review their partners' answers from A and rewrite their paragraphs if necessary.

Edit

C (15–20 minutes)

1. Direct students to read and complete the Self-Assessment checklist. They should be prepared to hand in their work or discuss it in class.

2. Ask for a show of hands for how many students gave all or mostly *Yes* answers.

3. Use the Unit Assignment Rubric on p. 12 in this *Teacher's Handbook* to score each student's assignment.

4. Alternatively, divide the class into large groups and have students read their paragraphs to their group. (Make copies of each student's writing for each person in the group, to assist with scoring.) Pass out copies of the Unit Assignment Rubric and have students score each other.

▶ *Reading and Writing 1, page 23*

Track Your Success (5 minutes)

1. Have students circle the words they have learned in this unit. Suggest that students go back through the unit to review any words they have forgotten.

2. Have students check the skills they have mastered. If students need more practice to feel confident about their proficiency in a skill, point out the pages numbers and encourage them to review.

3. Read the learning outcome aloud (*Write about a name you like, giving information about the name*). Ask students if they feel that they have met the outcome.

Unit Assignment Rubric

Student name: _____

Date: _____

Unit Assignment: *Write sentences about a name you like.*

20 = Writing element was completely successful (at least 90% of the time).
15 = Writing element was mostly successful (at least 70% of the time).
10 = Writing element was partially successful (at least 50% of the time).
 0 = Writing element was not successful.

Writing Sentences	20 points	15 points	10 points	0 points
Sentences have correct spelling and appropriate final punctuation.				
Sentences have subjects and verbs and they agree.				
Sentences correctly use the simple present.				
Sentences provide answers to the two questions *Where does the name you like come from?* and *Why do you like it?*				
Proper nouns are capitalized.				

Total points: _____

Comments:

Unit QUESTION
What is a good job?

Work

READING • previewing a text
VOCABULARY • word forms
WRITING • writing complete sentences
GRAMMAR • verbs + infinitives (*like, want,* and *need*)

LEARNING OUTCOME

Describe the duties of a job you want and give reasons that it is a good job for you.

▶ *Reading and Writing 1, page 25*
Preview the Unit

Learning Outcome

1. Ask for a volunteer to read the unit skills, then the unit learning outcome (*Describe the duties of a job you want and give reasons that it is a good job for you.*).

2. Explain: *This is what you are expected to be able to do by the unit's end. The learning outcome explains how you are going to be evaluated. With this outcome in mind, you should focus on learning these skills (Reading, Vocabulary, Writing, Grammar) that will support your goal of describing the duties of a job that you want and why it is a good job for you. This can also help you act as mentors in the classroom to help the other students meet this outcome.*

A (10 minutes)

1. To get students thinking about work and jobs, ask them some of the following questions: *What was your first job? What jobs are popular in this country? What jobs are popular in your country? What is your dream job? Why do people change jobs?* Have students answer questions in small groups or elicit answers in a class discussion.

2. Put students in pairs or small groups to discuss the first two questions in A.

3. Call on volunteers to share their ideas with the class. Ask questions: *What is your current job? What do you do at your job? Do you like your job? Why or why not? Why are jobs important to have?*

4. Focus students' attention on the photo. Have a volunteer describe the photo to the class. Read the third question aloud. Ask: *Why do the jobs in the photo look like good (or bad) jobs? Are these jobs busy or dull? What are they doing in the photo?* Elicit or supply needed vocabulary.

Activity A Answers, p. 25
Answers will vary. Possible answers:
1. Yes, I like to work. No, I don't like to work.
2. Yes, I have a job. No, I don't have a job. Yes, I do want a job.
3. Yes, their jobs look interesting. No, their jobs do not look interesting.

B (10 minutes)

1. Introduce the Unit Question, *What is a good job?* Ask related information questions or questions about personal experience to help students prepare for answering the more abstract unit question. For example, ask: *What makes your job good? What could make your job better? What duties would the perfect job include? What would make you leave your current job for a new job? What would make you quit your current job?* List the answers that students think of (e.g., *a good salary* or *a fair boss*) on the board. Help with vocabulary as needed. If most students do not work, have them consider jobs they would like to have.

2. Label four pieces of poster paper with four interesting answers to the question, *What makes your job good?* (e.g., *a good salary, more vacation, free lunch,* or *a fair boss*). Place each paper in a corner of the room.

3. Ask students to read and consider the Unit Question for a moment and then to stand in the corner next to the poster that best represents their answer to the question. If students stand by only one or two options, have some students stand by the answer that represents their second or third choice.

4. Direct the groups in each corner to talk among themselves about the reasons for their answers. Tell them to choose a secretary to record the answers on the poster paper.

5. Call on volunteers from each corner to share their opinions with the class.

6. Keep the posters for students to refer back to at the end of the unit.

> **Activity B Answers, p. 25**
> Answers will vary. Possible answers: A good job is fun. A good job has a good salary. Good jobs have good hours and treat people fairly.

The Q Classroom (5 minutes)
🔊 CD1, Track 05

1. Play The Q Classroom. Use the example from the audio to help students continue the conversation. Ask: *How did the students answer the question? Do you agree or disagree with their ideas? Why?*

2. Elicit all the elements of a good job that the students on the audio name. Replay the audio if needed. Are any of the elements the same as the ones the students listed on the poster boards? If there are new ones, discuss them and have students vote for the top one or two. Discuss the results. Which elements of a good job are most and least important for your class?

▶ *Reading and Writing 1, page 26*

C (15 minutes)

1. Draw a picture on the board of yourself teaching. Beside the picture write two professions: *a teacher* and *a banker*. Direct students to decide which profession is represented in the picture.

2. Have students complete Activity C individually and then check their answers with partners. Check answers as a class when groups are finished.

3. Place students into small groups and ask them to draw a picture of themselves doing their jobs. As students work, note professions being drawn. Provide help with drawings as needed. Encourage them to include *student* or *mom/dad* if they do not work.

4. Once all members of the group have drawn their pictures, pass the packet of drawings to another group. The new group has to appraise each drawing and write which profession is represented. Write professions (e.g., *gardener, computer technician, housecleaner,* or *construction worker*) on the board if students cannot come up with the nouns.

5. Share drawings and professions with the class. Model pronunciation of professions.

> **Activity C Answers, p. 26**
> **1.** salesclerk; **2.** construction worker;
> **3.** truck driver; **4.** chef; **5.** nurse; **6.** office worker

MULTILEVEL OPTION

Have lower-level students draw the pictures of their profession and have higher-level students help label them.

Have higher-level students add a sentence to their and their lower-level partner's drawings describing what each profession does.

D (10 minutes)

1. Pair students and have them ask each other questions.

2. Instruct students to share some of their answers to question 2 with the class. *Why are some of these jobs good? Why are some not good?*

> **Activity D Answers, p. 26**
> Answers will vary. Possible answers: A nurse is a good job because you help other people. Construction worker is a hard job because you work outside.

EXPANSION ACTIVITY: Find Someone Who…
(10 minutes)

1. Ask students to brainstorm a list of jobs that they currently have or have had in the past (e.g., clerical work, landscaping, or cooking).

2. Change the job names from verbs to nouns (e.g., *clerical worker, landscaper,* or *cook*) and write them on the board. Include your own job.

3. Have students draw a grid on a blank piece of paper that is two squares high and three squares long. In each square, have students write one profession, randomly chosen. Above the grid, have students write: *Are you a _____?*

4. Ask students to stand up and interview other students in class. They need to find other students in the class who do those professions by asking the question, "*Are you a _____?*" and inserting a profession (e.g., *Are you a baker?*).

5. When students find someone who answers *yes* to a question, that student must sign the interviewer's grid in the square where the profession is written. Each student's goal is to get all six squares signed. If a student answers *no* to a question, the student has to find a new student to interview. They can't ask one student two questions in a row.

▶ *Reading and Writing 1, page 27*

READING 1: The Right Job for You

VOCABULARY (15 minutes)

1. Write (or have students write) vocabulary definitions on eight pieces of large white paper. Assign one definition to each of eight students.

2. Photocopy sentences 1–8 and cut them into strips. Make enough copies so that each student has one sentence and all eight sentences are used. Have students underline the bolded vocabulary word in their sentences.

3. Instruct the eight students with vocabulary definitions to stand around the perimeter of the room with their definitions facing toward the middle of the classroom.

4. Tell the remaining students, with the sentences, to find the correct definition of their vocabulary word and stand with the person holding their definition. Monitor groupings to ensure that student make correct matchings.

5. When all students are matched correctly, have students say to the class (a) the sentence; (b) the definition of the vocabulary item; and, for repetition, (c) the word [*insert vocabulary item*] means [*insert definition*].

6. Have students return to their seats and transcribe the answers into their textbooks. Offer corrections as needed.

MULTILEVEL OPTION

For lower-level students, ensure that they are the ones holding the definitions. Have higher-level students match the sentences with the correct definition. Additionally, have higher-level students write an additional sentence for each vocabulary item and share them with a lower-level partner.

Vocabulary Answers, p. 27
a. plan; **b.** decision; **c.** career; **d.** outside;
e. success; **f.** solve; **g.** skill; **h.** creative

 For additional practice with the vocabulary, have students visit *Q Online Practice*.

▶ *Reading and Writing 1, page 28*

Reading Skill: Previewing a text (5 minutes)

1. Go over the reading skill at the top of the page with students. Elicit similarities between *previewing* and *scanning* a text.

2. Model meanings of *title, heading,* and *captions* using texts that you have with you such as this book, the student book, other books, newspapers, or magazines. To practice thinking of captions, have students think of captions to the photos on page 26. Have students share captions with the class.

3. Check comprehension by asking questions: *What is the title of your textbook? What's one heading you see on page 28 of your textbook? What is a caption?*

PREVIEW READING 1 (10 minutes)

1. Ask students to locate the title, headings, and captions in the article *Winter Hill Career Center*. Based upon a preview of those items alone, not from reading the entire article, ask students to answer questions 1–3.

2. Instruct students to check their answers with a partner. Check as a class as needed.

3. Tell students they should review their answers after reading.

Preview Reading 1 Answer, p. 28
1. b; **2.** a; **3.** b

Reading 1 Background Note

Personality tests have long been used as a predictor of vocational interest. In many U.S. schools, students take career aptitude tests that probe their personality types to determine a range of vocations that might be suitable for them. Such tests can be helpful for students who are not sure what field they want to enter.

The Myers-Briggs Type Indicator® (MBTI®) is a well-known personality assessment. The MBTI® looks at four pairings and makes a judgment of the test-takers overall personality type. Different groups then analyze that data and provide suggestions about what careers such personality types would be good at or enjoy. Do an Internet search for "Myers-Briggs" and see what kinds of tests you can find!

READParameter

 CD1, Track 06

1. Instruct students to read the article *Winter Hill Career Center*.

2. Play the audio and have students follow along.

▶ *Reading and Writing 1, page 30*

MAIN IDEAS (5 minutes)

1. Choose a student to read the directions aloud.

2. Ask students to read and complete the activity individually.

3. Check answers and discuss as a class.

> **Main Idea Answers, p. 30**
> a; d

Tip for Success (1 minute)

1. Draw students' attention to the Tip for Success.

2. Reiterate the importance of underlining or highlighting key words in questions *before* scanning a text for answers. Suggest they do this for the Details activity.

DETAILS (10 minutes)

1. Read the directions aloud to students. Direct students to read the career test and complete the activity.

2. Have students compare answers with a partner.

3. Direct students to look back at the article to check their answers.

4. Go over the answers with the class. Review the article as necessary.

> **Details Answers, p. 30**
> **1.** a; **2.** b; **3.** a; **4.** a; **5.** a; **6.** b

> **web** For additional practice with reading comprehension, have students visit *Q Online Practice*.

WHAT DO YOU THINK? (15 minutes)

1. Ask students to take the career test and reflect on their answers.

2. Seat students in small groups and assign roles: a group leader to make sure everyone contributes, a note-taker to record the group's ideas, a reporter to share the group's ideas with the class, and a timekeeper to watch the clock.

3. Give students five minutes to discuss the results of the career test and the questions and information in Step 2. Call time if conversations are winding down. Allow extra time if necessary.

4. Call on each group's reporter to share ideas with the class.

> **What Do You Think? Answers, p. 30**
> Answers will vary. Possible answers: I like to work outside, so I should be a construction worker. I like to talk, so I should be a lawyer. I'm good with numbers, so I should be an accountant.

Learning Outcome

Use the learning outcome to frame the purpose and relevance of Reading 1. Ask: *What did you learn from Reading 1 that prepares you to describe the duties of the job you want and give reasons that it is a good job for you?*

▶ *Reading and Writing 1, page 31*

READING 2: The World of Work

VOCABULARY (15 minutes)

1. Direct students to read the words and definitions in the box. Model pronunciation and have students repeat the words.

2. Have students work with a partner to complete the sentences. Call on volunteers to read the completed sentences aloud.

3. Have pairs create one new sentence for each vocabulary item.

4. Select model sentences and ask students to write them on the board. Practice group editing if necessary, using the first five items from the rubric on page 40.

> **Vocabulary Answers, p. 31**
> **1.** result; **2.** tour; **3.** regular;
> **4.** pay; **5.** duty; **6.** flexible

> **web** For additional practice with the vocabulary, have students visit *Q Online Practice*.

PREVIEW READING 2 (15 minutes)

1. Ask a student to read the directions. Have students work individually to preview questions in the article and check their ideas.

2. Ask: *Which of these topics are the people in the interviews not asked about? Why do you think they were not asked about these topics?*

3. Tell students they should review their answers after reading.

> **Preview Reading 2 Answers, p. 32**
> 2; 3; 6

Tip for Success (1 minute)

1. Ask a volunteer to read the Tip for Success.

2. Remind students to choose one key word a day to add to their personal dictionaries. Ask them to add any words from Reading 2 that they circled to their dictionaries, too.

Reading 2 Background Note

In the article *The World of Work*, the interviewees talked about many aspects of their jobs. However, they did not talk about their pay. Americans, among other groups of people, do not usually talk about how much they earn at their jobs. In fact, some people find the topic rude—even among friends. But why? One explanation is that money is simply something that people do not like to discuss. Do people really want to know that they make less than their friends? Conversely, do people want to brag that they make more than their friends? Sometimes, ignorance is bliss.

READ

 CD1, Track 07

1. Instruct students to read the article.

2. Play the audio and have students follow along.

MAIN IDEAS (5 minutes)

1. Read the directions to students and ask the class to vote on which answer is correct.

2. Have a student tally the votes.

> **Main Idea Answer, p. 33**
> b

DETAILS (5 minutes)

1. Direct students to preview the options and complete the activity.

2. Have students compare answers with a partner.

3. Direct students to look back at the article to check their answers.

4. Go over the answers with the class.

> **Details Answers, p. 33**
> **1.** c; **2.** d; **3.** a; **4.** b

 For additional practice with reading comprehension, have students visit *Q Online Practice*.

WHAT DO YOU THINK?

A (10 minutes)

1. Ask students to read the questions and reflect on their answers.

2. Seat students in small groups and assign roles: a group leader to make sure everyone contributes, a note-taker to record the group's ideas, a reporter to share the group's ideas with the class, and, if there are enough students, a timekeeper to watch the clock.

3. Give students five minutes to discuss the questions. Call time if conversations are winding down. Allow them an extra minute or two if necessary.

> **Activity A Answers, p. 34**
> Answers will vary. Possible answers: Flexible hours are important to me. Good pay at a job is important to me. Learning about electronics is not important to me.

B (10 minutes)

1. Tell the students that they should think about both Reading 1 and Reading 2 as they answer the questions in B. Students will answer each question by writing two or three sentences in response.

2. Ask students to read their sentences with a partner.

3. Call on each pair to share ideas with the class.

Learning Outcome

Use the learning outcome to frame the purpose and relevance of Readings 1 and 2. Ask: *What did you learn from Reading 2 that prepares you to describe the duties of the job you want and give reasons that it is a good job for you?*

Vocabulary Skill: Word forms (10 minutes)

1. Present the lesson on word forms and ask for volunteers to read the examples aloud.

2. Have students go back to the readings and look for and then circle the words in the table, either on their own or with a partner. Have them determine the part of speech and share their ideas with the class.

3. Check comprehension: *What clues are in the sentence that can help you figure out if a word is a noun or a verb?*

Skill Note

Noticing clues in sentences that can lead to an understanding of whether a word is a noun or a verb can be tricky—for students and teachers alike! Use the following "rules of thumb" to help guide student recognition of nouns and verbs.

1. Nouns are often preceded by articles and possessive pronouns.

2. Verbs are often preceded by pronouns and nouns.

A (10 minutes)

1. Write the "rules of thumb" from the Skill Note on the board, then provide or elicit some examples (e.g., Nouns are *a job, his boss,* or *the paycheck.* Verbs are *they work, the boss helps,* or *we are hardworking*). Define unknown grammatical terms—such as *possessive pronoun.* Ask students to use these rules to help them complete the activity.

2. Go over the answers with the class.

Activity A Answers, p. 35
1. N; **2.** N; **3.** V; **4.** V; **5.** N

B (10 minutes)

1. Ask students to stand up with books in hand.

2. Delineate one side of the classroom as "noun" and the other side as "verb."

3. Ask a volunteer to read a sentence. Students should move to the side of the classroom that conforms to their answer. Once students have chosen a side of the classroom, ask volunteers to explain the rationale for their choice. Refer students to the "rules of thumb" from the Skill Note as necessary.

4. Repeat process for the remaining four sentences.

Activity B Answers, p. 35
1. noun; **2.** verb; **3.** verb; **4.** noun; **5.** noun

 For additional practice with word forms, have students visit *Q Online Practice.*

Critical Thinking Tip (1 minute)

1. Read the tip aloud.

2. Remind students that writing a label on examples of things they have already learned can also be a useful study aid.

Critical Q: Expansion Activity

Label

1. Put students in groups and have them consider whose opinions they value about how well they work (e.g., self, friends, boss).

2. Focus students' attention on two opinion-makers: themselves and their bosses. Students who do not work can think of their teacher(s) instead of their bosses.

3. Draw a Venn diagram on the board—and have students copy it on a piece of paper. Label one circle *Self* and the other *Boss.*

4. Have students brainstorm work-related values that are important only to themselves (e.g., *hardworking* or *honest*). Place them in the *Self* bubble. Then have students brainstorm work-related values that are important only to their bosses (e.g., *quick* or *timely*). Place them in the *Boss* bubble.

5. Note which bubble holds more attributes. If it is the boss's side, ask: *Why do the boss's opinions matters more than their own?* If it is the self's side, ask: *Why are the boss's opinions not more valued?*

6. Have students think about which work-related values are important to both themselves and bosses. Place them in the middle of the Venn diagram.

▶ *Reading and Writing 1 page 36*

WRITING

Writing Skill: Writing complete sentences (15 minutes)

1. Ask for volunteers to read the text aloud. Stop them at logical points and provide additional explanation as needed and provide or elicit more examples. Correct pronunciation as necessary.

2. Tell students: *This is why we have been practicing recognizing nouns and verbs. You need to always ensure that your sentence has both, and to do that, you need to recognize what they are.*

3. Check comprehension. Write a few simple sentences and fragments on the board and ask students to identify the nouns and the verbs, or in the case of fragments, to identify which is missing, the noun or verb. Ask: *What makes a sentence complete? What makes a sentence a fragment?*

A (10 minutes)

1. Ask a volunteer to restate the "rules of thumb" from page 18 of this *Teacher's Handbook* that provide clues as to whether a word is a noun or a verb. Write the rules on the board if necessary.

2. Have a student read the directions for the activity. Review model sentence 1. Explain the rationale for the answer.

3. Have students complete the remaining sentences individually and compare their answers with a partner.

4. Go over the answers with the class. Elicit corrections as necessary.

Activity A Answers, p. 36
1. Underline: A truck driver / Circle: works;
2. Underline: He / Circle: drives;
3. Underline: Truck drivers / Circle: travel;
4. Underline: They / Circle: sleep;
5. Underline: The company / Circle: pays;
6. Underline: A driver / Circle: needs

▶ *Reading and Writing 1 page 37*

Tip for Success (1 minute)

1. Read the Tip for Success aloud.

2. Tell students that future assignments—both in and outside of this class—will often be graded or scored based on correct capitalization and punctuation.

B (10 minutes)

1. Read the directions and review the model answer. Point out that *work* is crossed out in the box because it was used in the model. Encourage students to cross out the words in the box as they use them. Field questions.

2. Have students complete the activity alone or in pairs. Alternatively, assign students the remaining sentences, one per student. Have students complete the sentence and check their answer with a partner who completed the same sentence. Monitor pairs to verify answers.

3. Place students into larger groups where each sentence is represented by a student. Have students share answers with the group.

Activity B Answers, p. 37
1. Nurses work in a hospital;
2. They wear white clothes in the hospital;
3. They don't make loud sounds in the hospital rooms;
4. The nurses follow the doctor's directions;
5. The nurses help the sick people;
6. The doctor visits the sick people every day.

 For additional practice with writing complete sentences, have students visit *Q Online Practice*.

Grammar: Verbs + infinitives (*like, want,* and *need*) (10 minutes)

1. Direct students to read the information.

2. Check comprehension by asking questions: Like, want, *and* need *are followed by which types of words? When a verb follows* like, want, *or* need, *what form does it take? What are some examples of noun phrases that you can think of?*

Skill Note

Noun phrases can be simply nouns that stand alone (e.g., *Tom, Colorado,* or *Mazda*) or nouns that are modified by articles (e.g., <u>*the* blue *Mazda*</u>), numbers (e.g., <u>*three* jobs</u>), possessives adjectives (e.g., <u>*his* boss</u>), adjectives, prepositional phrases (e.g., *two birds* <u>*by the shore*</u>), or relative clauses (e.g., *the book* <u>*that I wrote*</u>).

When a verb is placed after *like, want,* or *need,* that verb always takes the infinitive form. Thus, there is always a *to* between *like, want,* or *need* and the infinitive verb that follows it (e.g., *I like to work at night. I need to know your schedule.*).

▶ *Reading and Writing 1 page 38*

A (10 minutes)

1. Go over the directions and have students complete the task individually.

2. Put students in pairs to discuss their answers.

3. Call on volunteers to share their ideas with the class. Ask volunteers to stand when they hear an infinitive and raise their left arms in the air when there is a noun phrases <u>after</u> *like, want,* or *need.*

Activity A Answers, p. 38
1. Underline: good food / Circle: to be, to work;
2. Underline: good pay / Circle: to be, to solve, to work;
3. Underline: big trucks / Circle: to be, to work, to see;
4. Underline: an office worker, regular hours / Circle: to be

B (10 minutes)

1. Direct students to complete the sentences.

2. Put students in pairs to discuss their answers.

3. Choose volunteers to write their answers on the board.

Activity B Answers, p. 38

Answers will vary. Possible answers:

1. I like to work on sunny days;
2. I like to see hardworking people;
3. I don't like to work for mean bosses;
4. I don't like to work for little money;
5. I want to find a better job;
6. I want to visit my boss' big house;
7. I need to look for more hours at work;
8. I don't need to help my hardworking boss much.

 For additional practice with *like, want,* and *need,* have students visit *Q Online Practice.*

21ST CENTURY SKILLS

Businesses are looking for leaders, people who can take initiative and get work done. Leadership demands self-confidence. Help students increase their self-confidence by having them continually reevaluate what they are good at and how they can contribute meaningfully to the marketplace. There is a role for every player and the best players know their strengths (and can account for their weaknesses). Begin each class with an "I can" statement (e.g., *I can work hard. I can learn English. I can give clear directions.*). Continually confirm students' skills and don't allow them to talk negatively about themselves. Constructive self-criticism is okay, but students shouldn't become their own worst enemies. Confidence is built step by step over time. Help students take one step every day by asking students to evaluate what they "did right" that day in class or at work.

Q Unit Assignment: Write sentences about a job that's right for you

Unit Question (5 minutes)

Refer students back to the ideas they discussed at the beginning of the unit about what is a good job.

Reintroduce the posters that students created during Activity B from page 25. Cue students if necessary by asking specific questions about the content of the unit: *What makes your job good? What could make your job better? Which personality types are suited for which jobs? Which job would you like to have?* Read the direction lines for the assignment together to ensure understanding.

Learning Outcome

1. Tie the Unit Assignment to the unit learning outcome. Say: *The outcome for this unit is to describe the duties of the job that you want and give reasons that it is a good job for you. This Unit Assignment is going to let you practice your writing and editing skills by writing a short text about a job that's right for you. Describing why a job is right for you is an important way for you to discover why you are the right person for that kind of job. If you clearly understand why you are the right person for a particular job, you will more likely be able to convince a potential employer that you are indeed the right person for the job.*

2. Explain that you are going to use a rubric similar to their Self-Assessment checklist on p. 40 to grade their Unit Assignments. You can also share a copy of the Unit Assignment Rubric (on p. 22 of this *Teacher's Handbook*) with the students.

▶ *Reading and Writing 2 page 39*

Plan and Write

Brainstorm

A (10 minutes)

1. Direct students to complete Activity A with a partner and share answers with another pair.

2. Write on the board any new ideas generated by question 2.

Tip for Success (3 minutes)

1. Read the Tip for Success aloud.

2. Tell students that while there is some great information on the Internet regarding job duties, they should also watch out for websites that are not related to the task they are doing. Scanning and previewing text is a good way to eliminate websites that will not be helpful.

Plan

B (10 minutes)

1. Go over the directions. Answer questions.

2. Circulate and help as needed with vocabulary for job duties.

3. Encourage students to share their answers with a partner.

Write

C (20 minutes)

1. Instruct students to write their sentences. Remind them to use vocabulary items from the unit and the verbs *like, want,* and *need*. If appropriate, give students a specific number of vocabulary items they must use.

Alternative Unit Assignments

Assign or have students choose one of these assignments to do instead of, or in addition to, the Unit Assignment.

1. Talk to two people about their jobs. What do they do? What are their job duties? What do they like about their jobs? Write sentences about each person.

2. Work in a small group. Tell the other members of your group about the job you have today. Explain your job duties. Explain what you like about the job. Explain what you don't like about the job. Answer any questions the members of your group ask.

3. Choose a job that you want. Write a list of your skills that are good for that job. Use skills from the career test in Reading 1 and your own ideas. Then read the job and your list of skills to a partner. Does your partner think you are right for the job?

 For an additional unit assignment, have students visit *Q Online Practice*.

▶ *Reading and Writing 1 page 40*
Revise and Edit

Peer Review

A (15–20 minutes)

1. Pair students and direct them to read each other's work.

2. Ask students to answer the questions and discuss them.

3. Give students suggestions of helpful feedback: *I liked your writing because…. You only included two job duties. Can you be clearer why you like the job? I don't think you used as many vocabulary words as you needed to use. What else can you write about why it's a good job?*

Rewrite

B (15–20 minutes)

Students should review their partners' answers from A and rewrite their paragraphs if necessary.

Edit

C (15–20 minutes)

1. Direct students to read and complete the Self-Assessment checklist. They should be prepared to hand in their work or discuss it in class.

2. Ask for a show of hands for how many students gave all or mostly *Yes* answers.

3. Use the Unit Assignment Rubric on p. 22 in this *Teacher's Handbook* to score each student's assignment.

4. Alternatively, divide the class into large groups and have students read their sentences to their group. (Make copies of each student's writing for each person in the group, to assist with scoring.) Pass out copies of the Unit Assignment Rubric and have students score each other.

▶ *Reading and Writing 1, page 41*
Track Your Success (5 minutes)

1. Have students circle the words they have learned in this unit. Suggest that students go back through the unit to review any words they have forgotten.

2. Have students check the skills they have mastered. If students need more practice to feel confident about their proficiency in a skill, point out the pages numbers and encourage them to review.

3. Read the learning outcome aloud (*Describe the duties of a job you want and give reasons that it is a good job for you*). Ask students if they feel that they have met the outcome

Unit 2   Work

Unit Assignment Rubric

Student name: _____

Date: _____

Unit Assignment: *Write sentences about a job that's right for you.*

20 = Writing element was completely successful (at least 90% of the time).
15 = Writing element was mostly successful (at least 70% of the time).
10 = Writing element was partially successful (at least 50% of the time).
 0 = Writing element was not successful.

Writing Sentences	20 points	15 points	10 points	0 points
Sentences begin with a capital letter and end with appropriate punctuation.				
Sentences have both a subject and a verb and those elements agree.				
Sentences use vocabulary from the unit and words in sentences are spelled correctly.				
The verbs *like, need,* and *want* are used correctly.				
Sentences are complete and provide clear and specific details about why the job is right for the writer.				

Total points: _____

Comments:

Unit QUESTION
Why do people immigrate to other countries?

Long Distance

READING • skimming for the main idea
VOCABULARY • word roots
WRITING • connecting sentences with *and* and *but*
GRAMMAR • *there is / there are* and *there was / there were*

LEARNING OUTCOME

Explain how a place changed because of international immigration or culture.

▶ *Reading and Writing 1, page 43*
Preview the Unit

Learning Outcome

1. Ask for a volunteer to read the unit skills, then the unit learning outcome.

2. Explain: *This is what you are expected to be able to do by the unit's end. The learning outcome explains how you are going to be evaluated. With this outcome in mind, you should focus on learning these skills (Reading, Vocabulary, Writing, Grammar) that will support your goal of explaining how a place changed because of immigration or culture. This can also help you act as mentors in the classroom to help the other students meet this outcome.*

A (10 minutes)

1. For the ESL classroom: Ask some students where they were born. Ask them if there are many students from their home country living where they currently live. For the EFL classroom: Ask students if they've ever lived abroad or if they plan to in the future. Ask them where they would like to live.

2. Put students in pairs or small groups to discuss the first two questions.

3. Call on volunteers to share their ideas with the class. Ask: *Do you know someone who lives abroad? How do you know that those countries have a lot of immigration?*

4. Focus students' attention on the photo. Read the third question aloud. Have a volunteer describe the photo to the class. Ask them for clues they see in the picture that support their opinions. Ask probing questions: *How are these people dressed? Did they dress for a long trip? Are they carrying much luggage? Do you think they had a long trip? Are there mostly men or women in the photo?*

Activity A Answers, p. 43
Answers will vary. Possible answers:
1. They are looking for a different life. They are looking for work. They are moving to be with their families.
2. The United States, England, Russia, Egypt, Israel, Sweden, and others.
3. I think they're immigrating because they are carrying luggage. I think the reason they are immigrating is because they are looking for a newer, better life somewhere else.

B (10 minutes)

1. Introduce the Unit Question, *Why do people immigrate to other countries?* Ask related information questions or questions about personal experience to help students prepare for answering the more abstract unit question: *Did you immigrate to this country? What were your reasons for leaving your home country? What were your reasons for choosing your new country? What did you bring with you?*

2. Tell students: *Let's start off our discussion by listing reasons why people might immigrate. For example, we could start our list with* finding work *because many people look for jobs in new countries. But there are many other reasons why people immigrate. What else can we think of?*

3. Seat students in small groups and direct them to pass around a paper as quickly as they can, with each group member adding one item to the list. Tell them they have two minutes to make the lists and they should write as many words as possible.

4. Call time and ask a reporter from each group to read the list aloud.

5. Use items from the list as a springboard for discussion. For example: *From our lists, we see that people from other cultures may immigrate to be with family, to find a better life, or to escape bad situations. Why should we learn about and understand these reasons?*

Answers will vary. Possible answers: For work. To live with family. In order to provide a better life for a person's family.

The Q Classroom (5 minutes)

🔊 CD1, Track 08

1. Play The Q Classroom. Use the example from the audio to help students continue the conversation. Ask: *How did the students answer the question? Do you agree or disagree with their ideas? Why?*

2. On the audio, Felix says that people might immigrate because they are looking for work. Explore this idea further by eliciting things that make work in other countries more attractive than work in one's own country (e.g., salary, better hours, or better working conditions).

▶ *Reading and Writing 1, page 44*

C (5 minutes)

1. Ask for a volunteer to read the instructions. Point to the picture of the map in your book and connect the country name to the country with your finger as you tell students to *draw a line*. Have students repeat the country names after you as they draw the lines.

MULTILEVEL OPTION

Have lower-level students find and label their home country on the map if it is shown.

Have higher-level students write the adjective used to describe a person from that country, such as Kenyan or Bangladeshi and/or have higher-level students label the languages spoken in the highlighted countries.

D (5 minutes)

1. Read the directions aloud. Direct students to complete the activity with a partner. Point out that the entire world is not shown on the map. Mention also that the outlines of countries other than the ones listed in Activity C are not shown, so students may not be completely accurate when pointing to the location of certain countries. Tell them that that is fine and you will help them.

2. Circulate around the room and help students find country locations as needed.

Activity D Answers, p. 44

Answers will vary. Possible answers: England, Iceland, Italy, Peru, Saudi Arabia, United States, and others

E (5 minutes)

1. Ask a volunteer to read the instructions aloud. Have students discuss the questions with a partner.

2. As a follow-up to question 2, ask students if they could imagine living permanently in the countries they've visited. Ask what would be easy or difficult about immigrating.

Activity E Answers, p. 44

Answers will vary.

EXPANSION ACTIVITY: Country Bingo (10 minutes)

1. Ask students to brainstorm the names of 15–20 countries (using those in the book and those students can think of). Write those names on the board.

2. Instruct students to draw a three square by three square grid on a blank piece of paper. Model the grid on the board.

3. Inside of each square, students should write the name of a country from the list on the board. In total, students should have nine countries in their grids.

4. Write the names of each country on the board on a separate slip of paper and place the slips into a bag.

5. Draw one name at a time out of the bag and call it out. Have students mark the country on their grids.

6. Once students have three countries in a row, they should shout, "*BINGO!*" Then start a new round.

MULTILEVEL OPTION

Have lower-level students draw names from the bag and read them.

Have higher-level students locate the countries from his/her Bingo card on a map or state a reason why they think people from that country might immigrate to a new country.

READING

► *Reading and Writing 1, page 45*

READING 1: The World in a City

VOCABULARY (10 minutes)

1. Read the directions. Ask a student volunteer to read each vocabulary word and its definition.

2. Put students in pairs to compare answers. Elicit the answers from volunteers. Have students repeat the bolded vocabulary words.

3. Ask questions to help students connect with the vocabulary: *What is your neighborhood like? What's the population of the city we are currently in? Is there a market in this city?*

MULTILEVEL OPTION

Place students in mixed-ability pairs. The higher-level students can assist lower-level students in filling in the blanks and explain their understanding of the meaning of the words. Direct students to alternate reading the sentences aloud. Encourage them to help each other with pronunciation.

Vocabulary Answers, p. 45
1. mix;   **2.** market;   **3.** worldwide;   **4.** foreign;
5. million;   **6.** population;   **7.** neighborhood

 For additional practice with the vocabulary, have students visit *Q Online Practice.*

► *Reading and Writing 1, page 46*

PREVIEW READING 1 (5 minutes)

1. Direct students to read the directions individually and complete the activity.

2. Tell students they should review their answer after reading.

Preview Reading 1 Answer, p. 46
2

Reading 1 Background Note

Travel websites are a convenient source of demographic and cultural information about a wide range of countries. They can provide destination guides, history, tips for getting around, and maps. Many people find travel websites to be more useful than other reference materials because they are user-friendly and interactive.

Some travel websites have user reviews. Travelers can get ideas of where to go, what to see, and what previous travelers felt about those locations and what they had to offer. Looking for adventure? Travels websites can provide user-generated reviews of the best places to see museums, mountain bike, or even bungee jump. Do you enjoy a less intense vacation? Find the best, local, and hidden coffee shops; the cheapest and tastiest restaurants; and the sites only locals know about. Search "Travel Advisor" or "Travel Planning" in an Internet search engine to find websites that have this type of information. Search for your country as well as others!

READ

 CD1, Track 09

1. Instruct students to read the Web page.

2. Play the audio and have students follow along.

► *Reading and Writing 1, page 47*

Reading Skill:
Skimming for the main idea (10 minutes)

1. Go over the presentation for this skill. Check students' understanding of the information in the first paragraph before moving on to the tips for skimming.

2. Check comprehension by asking questions: *What is skimming? Do you ever do this in your daily life (e.g., skimming recipes to see what ingredients you'll need or skimming a newspaper page to see if there are any articles that interest you)? Why is skimming useful? What should you do first when you skim? What's next? Do you do this already? How will this skill be helpful for you as a student?*

 For additional practice with skimming, have students visit *Q Online Practice.*

Skill Note

Knowledge in academic settings is often transmitted through assigned reading texts. Teachers have reading lists, friends have book recommendations, and magazines and social websites are always a tempting diversion from a course's reading load. There simply isn't enough time in the day for students to read every word of every textbook assigned for every course. Student must read judiciously and with purpose. Skimming is one important means of accomplishing that task. Effective readers are those who can wring a text out like a sponge and soak up the important information. Skimming allows students to pinpoint what it is they need to soak up, section it off from less-important text, and process it. In an academic world where every minute counts, skimming can help make unmanageable reading lists less overwhelming. The sooner students master this skill, the more purposeful and successful their academic experience will be.

▶ *Reading and Writing 1, page 48*

MAIN IDEAS (5 minutes)

1. Tell students that if they are truly skimming, not reading, they should be able to answer the questions quickly.

2. Ask students to read and complete the activity individually.

3. Ask volunteers to share their answers. Check understanding by having students look back at the reading to confirm their answers.

> **Main Idea Answers, p. 48**
> **1.** c; **2.** a; **3.** b; **4.** b

DETAILS (5 minutes)

1. Direct students to circle the best answers to complete the activity.

2. Have students compare answers with a partner.

3. Direct the students to look back at the Web page to check their answers.

4. Go over the answers with the class.

> **Details Answers, p. 48**
> **1.** b; **2.** c; **3.** a; **4.** b; **5.** c

 For additional practice with reading comprehension, have students visit *Q Online Practice.*

Tip for Success (1 minute)

1. Read the Tip for Success.

2. Tell students they should try to read each answer in a multiple choice field before choosing their answer. Explain the following: *Sometimes answers are designed to trick you, so you want to ensure that you consider each answer before selecting the one you think is correct. Another good strategy is to eliminate one answer from the possible options. Thus, you are increasing the probability that you are selecting the correct answer by narrowing your chances from 1/4 to 1/3. Being right 33% of the time is better than being right 25% of the time.*

▶ *Reading and Writing 1, page 49*

WHAT DO YOU THINK? (20 minutes)

1. Ask students to read the questions and reflect on their answers.

2. Seat students in small groups and assign roles: a group leader to make sure everyone contributes, a note-taker to record the group's ideas, a reporter to share the group's ideas with the class, and a timekeeper to watch the clock.

3. Give students five minutes to discuss the questions. Call time if conversations are winding down. Allow them an extra minute or two if necessary.

4. Call on each group's reporter to share ideas with the class.

5. Have each student choose one of the questions and write two or three sentences in response.

6. Call on volunteers to share their ideas with the class.

> **MULTILEVEL OPTION**
>
> Have lower-level students read the questions aloud. For higher-level students, add the question *Why?* to the end of the first two discussion questions to encourage them to give more detailed responses.

> **What Do You Think? Answers, p. 49**
> Answers will vary.

Learning Outcome

Use the learning outcome to frame the purpose and relevance of Reading 1. Ask: *What did you learn from Reading 1 that prepares you to explain how a place changed because of international immigration?*

READING 2: Immigrant Stories

VOCABULARY (10 minutes)

1. Read the directions and check students' understanding by asking them what they need to do to complete the activity.

2. Ask for volunteers to give their answers and check to see that everyone agrees.

> **Vocabulary Answers, p. 50**
> **a.** community; **b.** support; **c.** lonely; **d.** own;
> **e.** opportunity; **f.** several; **g.** international

 For additional practice with the vocabulary, have students visit *Q Online Practice.*

▶ *Reading and Writing 1, page 50*

PREVIEW READING 2 (5 minutes)

1. Read the directions and check that students remember what they learned about skimming. Ask for a volunteer to remind everyone what skimming is and how it can be useful.

2. Tell students that you will enforce the time limit on this activity to ensure that they are skimming and not reading. After five minutes, call on volunteers to share their answers with the class. Ask students which words they saw when they were skimming that helped them to know the answers.

3. Tell students they should review their answers after reading.

   Preview Reading 2 Answers, p. 50
   1. T;   **2.** T;   **3.** F

Reading 2 Background Note

London is a cultural center of Europe (and the world), but it is also a bustling business hub. Many people come to London for job opportunities, and there are numerous sectors for people to find work in. Consider the following recent work-related statistics from the United Kingdom's Office of National Statistics:

Of 3.3 million workers:

Agriculture employs .33%

Construction employs 5.26%

Education employs 7.46%

Health and Social Work employs 10%

Manufacturing employs 7.6%

Real Estate employs 20%

READ

🔊 CD1, Track 10

1. Instruct students to read the stories.

2. Play the audio and have students follow along.

▶ *Reading and Writing 1, page 52*

MAIN IDEAS (5 minutes)

1. Read the directions aloud.

2. Ask students to read and complete the activity individually.

3. Ask for volunteers to share their answers and ask them to use evidence from the story to support their answers.

Main Idea Answers, p. 52
1. Yes;   **2.** Yes;   **3.** Yes;   **4.** Yes;   **5.** No;   **6.** No

Tip for Success (1 minute)

1. Read the Tip for Success.

2. Tell students that as they learn new material in a course, it is important that they apply skills learned earlier to new material.

▶ *Reading and Writing 1, page 53*

DETAILS (10 minutes)

1. Direct students to read the problems and successes and complete the activity.

2. Have students compare answers with a partner.

3. Direct the students to look back at the stories to check their answers.

4. Go over the answers with the class.

   Details Answers, p. 53
   Sun Yung Wing: 1, 2, 4, 5, 7, 8
   Basher Ali: 5, 6, 8
   Apara Asuquo: 3, 7

 For additional practice with reading comprehension, have students visit *Q Online Practice*.

WHAT DO YOU THINK?

A (10 minutes)

1. Ask students to read the questions and reflect on their answers.

2. Seat students in small groups and assign roles: a group leader to make sure everyone contributes, a note-taker to record the group's ideas, a reporter to share the group's ideas with the class, and a timekeeper to watch the clock.

3. Give students five minutes to discuss the questions. Call time if conversations are winding down. Allow them an extra minute or two if necessary.

4. Tell students to choose one question and write two or three sentences in response.

   Activity A Answers, p. 53
   Answers will vary. Possible answers:
   1. The language here is hard. There are not a lot of good jobs here now. Without their families, people are sad.
   2. I started my own business here. My children go to school here. Children are getting a good education so they will have good jobs.

B (10 minutes)

1. Tell the students that they should think about both Reading 1 and Reading 2 as they answer the questions in B.

2. Ask students to discuss the questions with a partner.

3. Call on each pair to share ideas with the class.

MULTILEVEL OPTION

For Activity A, have higher-level students write five or six sentences in response.

For Activity B, have lower-level students write out some of their answers before they tell them to a partner.

Critical Thinking Tip (1 minute)

1. Read the tip aloud.

2. Tell students that restating also helps to ensure that they have understood something correctly. After reading a new piece of information, they should try to restate it to a classmate who has also read the information, to ensure that they both have the same understanding of information.

Critical Q: Expansion Activity

Restate

1. Have students write or tell a personal story about their immigration experience—or the experience of someone they know who immigrated. (If they don't have personal stories, ask students to invent a story).

2. Pair students up and have each student read (or just tell) his or her story to the other student. Instruct students that they need to listen so that they can tell their partner's story to another student.

3. Once students feel prepared, pair them with a new partner. They must tell their new partner their previous partner's story of immigration.

Learning Outcome

Use the learning outcome to frame the purpose and relevance of Readings 1 and 2 and the Critical Q activity. Ask: *What did you learn from Reading 2 that prepares you to explain how a place changed because of international immigration or culture?*

▶ *Reading and Writing 1, page 54*

Vocabulary Skill: Word roots (5 minutes)

1. Go over the information on word roots.

2. Check comprehension: *What do each of the words in the word root list mean? Can you think of another word root? (e.g.,* act—*meaning* do *or* move—*as in* action, react, *and* activity). *How are word roots helpful to someone learning another language?*

Skill Note

Root words are packets of information embedded within larger words. Often, these words find their origins in other languages. Knowing these root words can help students recognize and process new words that contain the same root.

To take the idea of root words a step further, we can look at an academic word list. In 2000, Averil Coxhead compiled 570 word families that occur quite often in academic texts. Each family has a "headword." Once that headword is learned by a student, he or she can uncover the meaning of other words in the family. For example, once a student knows the word *adjust*, they can figure out the meanings of the following words: *adjusted, adjusting, adjustment, adjustments, adjusts, readjust, readjusted, readjusting, readjustment, readjustments,* and *readjusts.*

Breaking apart words into smaller units of meaning can help students better navigate text; understanding the meaning of those headwords and root words can lead to a greater comprehension of new words when considered in context.

A (5 minutes)

1. Direct students to work with a partner to match word roots to their definitions.

2. Go over the answers with the class.

> **Activity A Answers, p. 54**
> **1.** c; **2.** a; **3.** b; **4.** d

B (5 minutes)

1. Direct students to work on their own to match the words to their definitions. Have them check their answers with a partner.

> **Activity B Answers, p. 54**
> **1.** d; **2.** a; **3.** b; **4.** c

 For additional practice with word roots, have students visit *Q Online Practice.*

▶ *Reading and Writing 1, page 55*

21ˢᵀ CENTURY SKILLS

An important academic and professional skill is critical thinking and problem solving. What is one of the most common "problems" English language learners encounter every time they read? New vocabulary. In order to extract understanding from a text, students have to confront new vocabulary and figure out ways to consider meaning in context. Thus, students consult dictionaries, peers, and teachers. As well, students have to think creatively. They can ask themselves: *What part of this word have I seen before? What did it mean then? Where else can I find information that can unlock this word's mysteries?* Keep students' reading and thinking minds agile by giving them a challenge word (in context) each day and have them write it in their personal dictionaries. Have them critically examine it for root words, headwords, contextual clues, and other information that can help decode the word's meaning. Constant activation of these critical thinking skills can help students more efficiently tackle future texts and gives them practice with critical thinking and problem solving.

WRITING

▶ *Reading and Writing 1, page 55*

Writing Skill: Connecting sentences with *and* and *but* (5 minutes)

1. Ask two higher-level students to read the introduction and examples.

2. Check comprehension: *When can you use* and *to connect sentences? When can you use* but? *When do we use commas with* and *and* but? (Answer: When *and* or *but* comes between two complete sentences.)

A (5 minutes)

1. Read the directions aloud. Direct students to complete the activity individually.

2. When finished, they should check their answers with a partner.

3. Go over the answers as a class and ask a volunteer to explain the reason for *and* or *but* for each sentence.

> **Activity A Answers, p. 55**
> **1.** and; **2.** but; **3.** but;
> **4.** and OR but; **5.** but; **6.** and

B (5 minutes)

Tell students to write complete sentences by connecting the two shorter sentences with *and* or *but*. Go over the answers with the class.

> **Activity B Answers, pp. 55–56**
> **1.** Ana likes England, but she wants to visit Mexico;
> **2.** There are not many Chinese people here, and Chang is lonely;
> **3.** There is a lot of world music in London, but there is a lot of English music too;
> **4.** There are not many Mexicans in New York City, but there are many immigrants from the Dominican Republic;
> **5.** She really wants to work, but she doesn't have a job.

 For additional practice connecting sentences with *and* and *but*, have students visit *Q Online Practice.*

▶ *Reading and Writing 1, page 56*

Grammar: *There is / there are* and *there was / there were* (10 minutes)

1. Read the description of the grammar point aloud. Ask for volunteers to read the sample sentences. Point out that we use *there is* for one item (singular nouns) and non-count nouns, and we use *there are* for plural nouns.

2. Check comprehension by asking questions: *What's the difference between* there is *and* there are? *Can you give me an example of a* there + be *sentence in the simple present? And in the simple past? How do you make a* there + be *sentence negative? Can you give me an example?*

Skill Note

This structure allows certain sentences to remain grammatically accurate by standing in as a "subject" for the sentence. So instead of saying, *That sentence has several errors,* one could say, *There are several errors in that sentence.*

Why does existential *there* exist if we can craft sentences that have both a subject and a verb? In some genres, like newspaper reporting, sentences need to be constructed that do not place blame for an action on any agent in the sentence. For example, police reports might state that *there was an incident on Friday night (by a man)* instead of *A man caused an incident Friday night.* The sentence focuses on the action and not on the doer of the action. If necessary, the doer can be placed at the end of a sentence.

Have students practice this concept by putting a number of sentences of the board that show one person as the "doer" of an action (e.g., *The dog attacked a child on my street yesterday* or *A car smashed into an apartment*). Have students rewrite these sentences using *there + be* (e.g., *There was a child on my street attacked by a dog yesterday* or *There was an accident at an apartment involving a car*).

(10 minutes)

1. Direct students to circle the correct verbs.
2. Put students in pairs to discuss their answers.
3. Call on volunteers to share their ideas with the class.

> **Activity Answers, pp. 56–57**
>
> | | | |
> |---|---|---|
> | **1.** were; | **2.** was; | **3.** were; |
> | **4.** are; | **5.** are; | **6.** are; |
> | **7.** are; | **8.** are; | **9.** is; |
> | **10.** are; | **11.** is; | **12.** is |

▶ *Reading and Writing 1, page 57*

Unit Assignment: Write sentences about a place that is changing

Unit Question (5 minutes)

Refer students back to the ideas they discussed at the beginning of the unit about why people immigrate to other countries. Cue students if necessary by asking specific questions about the content of the unit: *What reasons did we discuss that cause people to immigrate? Why have people you know immigrated? If you've immigrated, why have you done so? How do immigrants change a country?* Read the direction lines for the assignment together to ensure understanding.

Learning Outcome

1. Tie the Unit Assignment to the unit learning outcome. Say: *The outcome for this unit is to explain how a place changed because of international immigration or culture. This Unit Assignment is going to let you show your skill in writing sentences about a place that's changing.*

2. Explain that you are going to use a rubric similar to their Self-Assessment checklist on p. 58 to grade their Unit Assignment. You can also share a copy of the Unit Assignment Rubric (on p. 32 of this *Teacher's Handbook*) with the students.

Plan and Write

Brainstorm

A (5 minutes)

Read the directions aloud. Direct students to brainstorm independently. Call time when it appears that most students are finished.

Your Writing Process (1 minute)

1. Read the Your Writing Process tip aloud.
2. Encourage students to use *Q Online Practice* frequently.

Plan

B (10 minutes)

Ask for a volunteer to read the directions aloud. Remind students that the Unit Assignment is a good place for them to practice using the new vocabulary and grammar skills they have learned in this unit—and that using unit vocabulary will help raise their Unit Assignment score. Direct students to complete the sentences using information they brainstormed in A.

▶ *Reading and Writing 1, page 58*

Write

C (15 minutes)

1. As students complete B, direct them to silently read the directions for C and complete the activity. Caution them not to simply rewrite the sentences they completed in B.

Alternative Unit Assignments

Assign or have students choose one of these assignments to do instead of, or in addition to, the Unit Assignment.

1. Write a guide to your town or city. (Look at Reading 1 as a model.) What are the interesting sights? Write about the interesting places a person can visit in your town. Write about the restaurants, markets, museums, and festivals.

2. Interview an immigrant in your area. Write the person's responses to these questions and other questions of your own.
   a. Why did you come here?
   b. Are you happy you are here?

c. Is your family with you? If not, where
are they?

d. Do you plan to stay? Why or why not?

 For an additional unit assignment, have students
visit *Q Online Practice*.

Revise and Edit

Peer Review

A (15–20 minutes)

1. Pair students and direct them to read each
other's work.

2. Ask students to answer the questions and
discuss them.

3. Give students suggestions of helpful feedback:
*The first two sentences give me a good idea of how
this city has changed. When you use* but *you should
be connecting two sentences that give different
information. You don't say too much about what the
place was like in the past.*

Tip for Success (3 minutes)

1. Read the Tip for Success aloud.

2. Briefly discuss why reading their own writing
aloud may help them find mistakes more quickly.

Rewrite

B (15–20 minutes)

Students should review their partners' answers from
A and rewrite their paragraphs if necessary.

Edit

C (15–20 minutes)

1. Direct students to read and complete the Self-
Assessment checklist. They should be prepared to
hand in their work or discuss it in class.

2. Ask for a show of hands for how many students
gave all or mostly *Yes* answers.

3. Use the Unit Assignment Rubric on p. 32 in
this *Teacher's Handbook* to score each student's
assignment.

4. Alternatively, divide the class into large groups
and have students read their sentences to their
group. (Make copies of each student's writing fpr
each person in the group, to assist with scoring.)
Pass out copies of the Unit Assignment Rubric
and have students grade each other.

▶ *Reading and Writing 1, page 59*

Track Your Success (5 minutes)

1. Have students circle the words they have learned
in this unit. Suggest that students go back through
the unit to review any words they have forgotten.

2. Have students check the skills they have mastered.
If students need more practice to feel confident
about their proficiency in a skill, point out the
pages numbers and encourage them to review.

3. Read the learning outcome aloud (*Explain how a
place changed because of international immigration
or culture*). Ask students if they feel that they have
met the outcome.

Unit 3　Long distance

Unit Assignment Rubric

Student name: _____

Date: _____

Unit Assignment: *Write sentences about a place that is changing.*

20 = Writing element was completely successful (at least 90% of the time).
15 = Writing element was mostly successful (at least 70% of the time).
10 = Writing element was partially successful (at least 50% of the time).
 0 = Writing element was not successful.

Writing Sentences	20 points	15 points	10 points	0 points
Sentences have both a subject and a verb and those elements agree.				
Sentences begin with capital letters and end with appropriate punctuation.				
Writing uses vocabulary from the unit and provides clear and specific details about a place that is changing.				
The use of *there + be* is correct in the present and past tense.				
Sentences connected with *and* and *but* are correct.				

Total points: _____

Comments:

4

Unit QUESTION
What are the benefits of positive thinking?

Positive Thinking

READING • making inferences
VOCABULARY • phrasal verbs
WRITING • using time order words to write a story
GRAMMAR • simple past

LEARNING OUTCOME

Write about a time when you or someone you know changed a situation with positive thinking.

▶ *Reading and Writing 1, page 61*
Preview the Unit

Learning Outcome

1. Ask for a volunteer to read the unit skills then the unit learning outcome *(Write about a time when you or someone you know changed a situation with positive thinking).*

2. Explain: *This is what you are expected to be able to do by the unit's end. The learning outcome explains how you are going to be evaluated. With this outcome in mind, you should focus on learning these skills (Reading, Vocabulary, Writing, Grammar) that will support your goal of writing about a time when you or someone you know changed a situation with positive thinking. This can also help you act as mentors in the classroom to help the other students meet this outcome.*

A (10 minutes)

1. Ask students: *What is "positive thinking"? Do you think positively? Do you know people who think positively? Maybe when they are in a bad situation, they try to think about good outcomes. For example, if a student is taking a difficult exam, he or she will think positively about passing that exam. What do you think? Today we're going to talk about the topic of positive thinking.*

2. Put students in pairs or small groups to discuss the first question in A.

3. Call on volunteers to share their ideas with the class. Ask questions: *Have you changed a situation with positive thinking? How would that situation be different if you had not thought positively? What is the difference between positive thinking and negative thinking? Is there anyone who doesn't believe the power of positive thinking? Please tell us why.*

4. Focus students' attention on the photo. Have a volunteer describe the photo to the class. Read the question aloud. Ask students to look at the photo. Ask them: *What do you see? What does the photo tell us about this woman's thinking? Is it positive or negative?* Explain to students: *This woman took an umbrella when she went outside. She thought it would rain, but it is not raining.* Ask: *Do you think she had positive or negative thinking when she went outside today? Why?* Have students share answers with partners. Ask: *Is being ready for bad situations the same thing as negative thinking?*

Activity A Answers, p. 61
Answers will vary. Possible answers:
1. Yes, I know a person with a positive way of thinking. My friends always try to see the good in every situation. No, I don't know a person with a positive way of thinking. My brother always thinks the worst will happen.
2. I see a woman. I see a green umbrella. It is not raining outside.

B (10 minutes)

1. Introduce the Unit Question, "What are the benefits of positive thinking?" Ask related information questions or questions about personal experience to help students prepare for answering the more abstract Unit Question. For example, ask: *When in your life have you used positive thinking? How did positive thinking help you in those situations? What stories have you heard about people who always think positively or always think negatively?*

2. Read the Unit Question aloud. Write these two options on the board: *1) Positive Thinking Can Change a Situation; 2) Positive Thinking Cannot Change a Situation.* Tell students they need to choose which answer they agree with more.

Give them a minute to silently consider their answers. Then ask students who would choose option number one to stand on one side of the room and students who would choose option number two to stand on the other side of the room.

3. Direct students to tell a partner next to them their reasons for choosing that side of the issue.

4. Call on volunteers from each side to share their opinions with the class.

5. After students have shared their opinions, provide an opportunity for anyone who would like to change sides to do so.

6. Ask students to sit down, copy the Unit Question, and make a note of their answers and their reasons. They will refer back to these notes at the end of the unit.

Activity B Answers, p. 61
Answers will vary. Possible answers: Positive thinking helps us get good results from different situations. People can make good things happen with positive thinking. There are no benefits to positive thinking. People control situations with actions, not with thinking.

The Q Classroom (5 minutes)
CD1, Track 11

1. Play The Q Classroom. Use the example from the audio to help students continue the conversation. Ask: *How did the students answer the question? Do you agree or disagree with their ideas? Why?*

2. Ask students: *Sophy mentions that positive thinking can make people happier. Do you agree? Why or why not? When in your life has positive thinking made you happier?*

▶ *Reading and Writing 1, page 62*

C (15 minutes)

1. Have the students complete the quiz individually. Circulate around the room answering questions as they arise.

2. Pair students and have them compare answers. Then, discuss answers as a class.

3. Have students check their favorite saying from the area below the quiz.

Activity C Answers, p. 62
1. e; **2.** d; **3.** a; **4.** f; **5.** c; **6.** b

D (5 minutes)

1. Put students in small groups to discuss questions 1–3. Remind them that everyone should have a chance to answer each question. As a class, ask for volunteers to share a few responses for each question.

READING

▶ *Reading and Writing 1, page 63*
READING 1:
The Power of Positive Thinking?

VOCABULARY (15 minutes)

1. Ask volunteers to read each of the vocabulary items plus their definitions. Elicit or provide sample phrases or sentences. Model pronunciation as necessary. Point out that *work out* is different from *workout*, meaning to do fitness exercises.

2. After students read the definitions, have students, in pairs, try to place each vocabulary item into sentences 1–8. Ask students to cross out or otherwise mark used vocabulary items as they fill in the sentences.

3. Correct answers as a class.

> **MULTILEVEL OPTION**
>
> Group lower-level students and assist them with the task. Provide alternate example sentences to help them understand the words, for example: *He **expects** me to be home soon. They **expect** class to be exciting. I'll **find out** the answer for you. She needs to **find out** who sent her the letter. You can't **give up** because you're almost done. Many people do not like to **give up** their dreams. If everything **works out**, we'll graduate on time. This semester will **work out** well if I get a good grade.*
>
> Have higher-level students complete the activity individually and then compare answers with a partner. Tell the pairs to write an additional sample sentence for each expression.

Vocabulary Answers, p. 63
1. find out; **2.** expect; **3.** knowledge;
4. work out; **5.** event; **6.** give up;
7. attitude; **8.** likely

 For additional practice with the vocabulary, have students visit *Q Online Practice*.

PREVIEW READING 1 (5 minutes)

1. Ask a volunteer to read the directions aloud.

2. Direct students to preview the reading, noting the title and the headings, and then answer the question.

3. Tell students they should review their answer after reading.

> **Preview Reading 1 Answer, p. 64**
> Yes

Reading 1 Background Note

When people watch athletes in person or on television, they might think to themselves, "How do they perform so well under such pressure?" As Judy McDonald, a researcher at the University of Ottawa in Canada notes, athletes often practice *visualization*. In other words, they visualize, or imagine, positive outcomes as they compete in their sports.

Often, when athletes tackle a problem (like making a key shot in a basketball game), they tell themselves, "Don't miss. Don't miss." However, that doesn't create an opportunity for the player to *not miss*. Instead, it does the opposite—it creates a mental image of the player missing! Instead, the person should be telling him/herself, "Make the shot! Make the shot!" Maintaining positive images, in the face of all challenges, can help people create their own positive outcomes.

READ

 CD1, Track 12

1. Instruct students to read the article, *The Power of Positive Thinking?*

2. Play the audio and have students follow along.

Tip for Success (1 minute)

1. Read the Tip for Success.

2. Have students take a note card and practice skimming Reading 1 using the edge of the card as a guide. If they don't have a note card, have them fold over a piece of paper and use that.

MAIN IDEAS (10 minutes)

1. Read the directions as a class. Complete the first statement as a class.

2. Ask students to read and complete the activity individually.

3. On the board, write "T = 1 finger" and "F = 2 fingers." Tell students you are going to check their answers without them saying a word. Direct students to hold up one finger if they responded "true" and two fingers on one hand if they responded "false." If there are many students holding up the incorrect number of fingers, stop to discuss using examples from the article.

> **Main Idea Answers, p. 65**
> **1.** T; **2.** F; **3.** T; **4.** F; **5.** T; **6.** F

DETAILS (15 minutes)

1. Direct students to read the quotes and complete the activity.

2. Have students compare answers with a partner.

3. Direct the students to look back at the article to check their answers.

4. Go over the answers with the class.

5. Ask students: *What about each quote you read made you think it was a positive quote? What about the quotes that you didn't think were positive?*

> **Details Answers, p. 65**
> Checked: 1, 3, 4, 6, 8

 For additional practice with reading comprehension, have students visit *Q Online Practice*.

Critical Thinking Tip (1 minute)

1. Read the tip aloud.

2. Explain to students that utilizing new information is a useful skill in speech as well as writing.

Critical Q: Expansion Activity

Utilizing information in a new situation
(10 minutes)

1. Explain to students: *"The Lost Horse" reminds us that bad news might not remain bad news. Things may be "a blessing in disguise." It takes a discerning eye to find the good news in the bad. On the other hand, it takes a critical mind to find the bad in what seems to be good. Let's apply this lesson to a new context.*

2. Bring in "junk mail" from home, if possible, or ask students to think about "junk mail" they've received. Remind students of credit card applications, for example, that promise 0% interest. On the surface, it appears to be free money. Direct students to think about "the catch." Remind them: *If it seems to good to be true, it probably is.*

3. Provide students with examples of "too good to be true" offers (e.g., $0 down payments; 0% interest credit card checks, etc). Develop a series of questions with students to encourage them to question offers that appear "too good to be true."

4. Point out to students that occasionally junk mail contains helpful things such as coupons and discounts at local businesses. These offers can be good and actually save people money. Thus, some 'bad' junk mail might actually turn out to be good.

Learning Outcome

Use the learning outcome to frame the purpose and relevance of Reading 1. Ask: *What did you learn from Reading 1 that prepares you to write about a time when you or someone you know changed a situation with positive thinking? What did you learn that will help you write about a time when you or someone you know changed a situation with positive thinking?*

▶ *Reading and Writing 1, page 66*
Reading Skill:
Making inferences (10 minutes)

1. Present the reading skill. Before class or when you teach this skill, think of additional statements and write them on the board. Have students provide appropriate inferences about them. This can be a written or oral activity.

2. Check comprehension by asking questions: *How is an inference different from a statement? When do you make inferences? Can you provide other statements and make inferences about them?*

A (15 minutes)

1. Ask a volunteer to read the directions. To check their understanding, ask the class: *What do you need to do now?*

2. Check answers as a class. Review the definition of *inference* and provide explanations for any wrong answers. For example: *"Positive people like work to be easy"* is not an inference because the reading doesn't cause us to guess that this fact is true.

   Reading Skill A Answers, p. 66
   1. a; **2.** b; **3.** b; **4.** a

B (5 minutes)

1. Direct students to work individually to put a check mark next to their inferences.

2. When finished, they should compare their answers with a partner and discuss any discrepancies.

3. Call on volunteers to share their responses with the class.

   Reading Skill B Answers, p. 66
   1; 3

 For additional practice with making inferences, have students visit *Q Online Practice*.

▶ *Reading and Writing 1, page 67*
WHAT DO YOU THINK? (20 minutes)

1. Ask students to read the activities and reflect on their answers.

2. Seat students in small groups and assign roles: a group leader to make sure everyone contributes, a note-taker to record the group's ideas, a reporter to share the group's ideas with the class, and a timekeeper to watch the clock.

3. Give students five minutes to discuss questions 1 and 2. Call time if conversations are winding down. Allow them extra time if necessary.

4. Call on each group's reporter to share ideas with the class.

5. Have students complete number 3.

   What Do You Think? Answers, p. 67
   Answers will vary.

Reading and Writing 1, page 68

READING 2: The Lost Horse

VOCABULARY (15 minutes)

1. Select a student to read the section heading and directions.

2. Read each vocabulary word aloud and have students repeat your pronunciation. Check for understanding of the words.

3. Assign each student a number (for example, 1–25 if there are 25 students) and have students with an odd number answer the odd-numbered vocabulary items, while students with an even number address the even-numbered items.

4. Odd-numbered students should check their answers with another odd-numbered student; even-numbered students should do the same.

5. Then pair an odd-numbered student with an even-numbered student and have them "teach" their vocabulary to the one another.

6. Check answers as a class.

> **Vocabulary Answers, p. 68**
> **1.** war; **2.** wise; **3.** run away; **4.** farm; **5.** wild;
> **6.** government; **7.** nation; **8.** send

 For additional practice with the vocabulary, have students visit *Q Online Practice*.

 Reading and Writing 1, page 69

PREVIEW READING 2 (5 minutes)

1. Direct students to read the directions and questions and think about their answers.

2. Tell students they should review their answer after reading.

Reading 2 Background Note

"The Lost Horse" is an old Chinese folktale. This tale reminds us that though something may appear bad at the time, it may turn out for the best in the end. Many folktales teach similar morals.

READ

 CD1, Track 13

1. Instruct students to read "The Lost Horse."

2. Play the audio and have students follow along.

 Reading and Writing 1, page 70

MAIN IDEAS (5 minutes)

1. Ask for a volunteer to read the heading and directions.

2. Ask students to read and complete the activity individually.

3. When students are finished, discuss the answers as a class. Ask students for examples from the story that support their answer.

> **Main Idea Answers, p. 70**
> **1.** b; **2.** c

DETAILS (15 minutes)

A (10 minutes)

1. Have students read the directions. Point out the sample answer. Then have the students put the remaining four details in order.

2. Have students compare answers with a partner.

3. Direct the students to look back at the story to check their answers.

4. Go over the answers with the class.

> **Activity A Answers, p. 70**
> **a.** 4; **b.** 2; **c.** 5; **d.** 1; **e.** 3; **f.** 6

B (5 minutes)

1. Direct students to read the sentences and complete the activity.

2. Have students compare answers with a partner.

3. Direct the students to look back at the story to check their answers.

> **Activity B Answers, p. 70**
> Answers will vary. Possible answers: 1, 3, 5, 7

 For additional practice with reading comprehension, have students visit *Q Online Practice*.

Moving on and learning from troublesome experiences is something that students will need to do in their academic and professional lives. Things don't always go according to plan in the classroom or the workplace. Accidents happen. Unfairness exists. Professionals have to quickly think of a "Plan B" when "Plan A" falls apart.

The ability to move on from a negative situation and work with others to come up with alternative solutions is an invaluable skill in the workplace. Positive thinking, and the ability to say to oneself, "That didn't work out, but I'm confident that I can come up with something that will" shows employers that you have the right attitude to succeed.

▶ *Reading and Writing 1, page 71*
WHAT DO YOU THINK?

A (10 minutes)

1. Ask students to read the questions and reflect on their answers.

2. Seat students in small groups and assign roles: a group leader to make sure everyone contributes, a note-taker to record the group's ideas, a reporter to share the group's ideas with the class, and, if there are enough students, a timekeeper to watch the clock.

3. Give students five minutes to discuss the questions. Call time if conversations are winding down. Allow them an extra minute or two if necessary.

4. Call on some of the reporters to share answers.

> **Activity A Answers, p. 71**
> Answers will vary. Possible answers:
> 1. I have to pay a lot of taxes. People ask me for money. The money causes a lot of unwanted attention.
> 2. A faster bus comes along after the first bus. I meet a new friend who offers me a ride. The bus crashes, but I am not on it.

B (5 minutes)

1. Tell the students that they should think about both Reading 1 and Reading 2 as they answer the questions in B. Ask students to choose one of the questions and write 3–5 sentences in response.

2. Ask students to read their sentences with a partner.

3. Call on each pair to share ideas with the class.

> **Activity B Answers, p. 71**
> Answers will vary. Possible answers:
> 1. His way of thinking is not positive or negative. Reading 1 shows that people can affect their situations with positive thinking. The wise old man shows that good outcomes may occur naturally.
> 2. Positive thinkers believe they can control what happens to them. Negative thinkers do not.

EXPANSION ACTIVITY: Against the Wall (10 minutes)

1. Ask the following question in relation to What Do You Think, question 1: Is the old man a positive thinker? Give students a minute to silently consider their answers to the question. Then ask students who would answer "yes" to stand on one side of the room and students who would answer "no" to stand on the other side of the room.

2. Direct students to tell a partner next to them their reasons for choosing that side of the issue.

3. Call on volunteers from each side to share their opinions with the class.

4. After students have shared their opinions, provide an opportunity for anyone who would like to change sides to do so.

5. Have students explain why they changed sides, if they did.

Learning Outcome

Use the learning outcome to frame the purpose and relevance of Readings 1 and 2. Ask: *What did you learn from Reading 2 that prepares you to write about a time when you or someone you know changed a situation with positive thinking?*

Vocabulary Skill: Phrasal verbs (10 minutes)

1. Present the material on phrasal verbs to students. Ask volunteers to read sentences aloud.

2. Have students, in pairs or individually, write sentences using each of the phrasal verbs in this description (*look after, look for, look out,* and *look through*). Circulate around the room and offer corrections as needed.

3. Have volunteers write their sentences on the board. Point out how the preposition changes the meaning of each phrasal verb combination and means something different from the original verb. Emphasize that phrasal verbs often have different definitions than the root verb.

4. Check comprehension by asking questions: *What is a phrasal verb? How is it different from an infinitive verb? Had you heard about phrasal verbs before today? What are some phrasal verbs you already know? Do you know these phrasal verbs:* give up, get out, go away? *What do you think each of these phrasal verbs means?*

Skill Note

Phrasal verbs are especially difficult for students because they can't look up each word individually and understand the meaning of the compound. In a phrasal verb, a verb is combined with a preposition (such as *up, down,* or *away*).

One way to determine which prepositions come with particular verbs is to search on the Internet for a website containing English language corpus. Enter the words "English corpus" or "corpus of American English" to find it. Once on a corpus website, you can enter a particular verb into the search box and ask the program to find which prepositions it usually goes with. Being presented with the common phrasal verb patterns for often-used verbs is one way for students to become familiar with phrasal verbs.

▶ *Reading and Writing 1, page 72*

A (5 minutes)

1. Direct students to match the phrasal verbs with their definitions.
2. Go over the answers with the class.

> **Activity A Answers, p. 72**
> **1.** c; **2.** f; **3.** b; **4.** e; **5.** d; **6.** a

B (10 minutes)

1. Direct students to read the sentences and complete the activity by choosing the correct phrasal verb from Activity A.
2. Go over the answers with the class.

> **Activity B Answers, p. 72**
> **1.** speak up; **2.** come over; **3.** give up;
> **4.** calm down; **5.** find out; **6.** slow down

C (5 minutes)

1. Direct students to complete the activity individually. Circulate around the classroom to answer questions or offer corrections as needed.
2. Have students share their answers in groups of 2–3.

> **Activity C Answers, p. 72**
> Answers will vary.

 For additional practice with phrasal verbs, have students visit *Q Online Practice.*

WRITING

▶ *Reading and Writing 1, page 73*

Grammar: Simple past (10 minutes)

1. Write *simple past* on the board and ask students what they know about it (e.g., see if they can contrast it with the simple present, and if they recognize the word *past*). Tell students that they will learn some rules for how to form verbs in the simple past. Direct students to read aloud the rules for the simple past one at a time, then stop and elicit or provide additional examples.

2. Check comprehension by asking questions: *What's the past form of* open? *Why is* studied *the past form of* study? *What's the past of* eat? *Is it regular or irregular?* Drill students on some of the common irregular verbs such as *to be, to eat,* and *to go.*

A (10 minutes)

1. Direct students to read the directions and complete the activity.
2. Have students check the answers in small groups.

> **Activity A Answers, p. 73**
> **1.** broke; **2.** came; **3.** fell; **4.** got; **5.** had;
> **6.** ran; **7.** said; **8.** sent; **9.** took

▶ *Reading and Writing 1, page 74*

B (10 minutes)

Ask a volunteer to read the directions. Direct students to fill in the blanks to complete the activity. Have students compare their answers with a partner, then check as a class.

> **Activity B Answers, p. 74**
> **1.** went; **2.** took; **3.** had; **4.** took, ran;
> **5.** lost; **6.** said

 For additional practice with regular and irregular simple past verbs, have students visit *Q Online Practice.*

1. Give students one minute to list as many past tense irregular verbs as they can think of. Check answers as a class.

2. Point out that many English learner's dictionaries have a list of irregular verb forms in an appendix. If possible, show them an example.

Writing Skill: Using time order words to write a story (5 minutes)

1. Read the heading and presentation aloud. Ask for volunteers to read the sample time order words.

2. Check comprehension by asking questions: *What are the time order words in the sentence, "A month later, the horse came back"? What is the time order word in, "He arrived a few minutes late"? What are some other time order words you know?*

Skill Note

Time order, or chronological, words help the reader understand how events relate to one another with regard to time. A simple way for students to practice using time order words in their writing is to write out step-by-step instructions for completing a task or to make a list of activities in their morning routine (e.g., *First, turn off the alarm. Five minutes later, turn on the shower. The next thing to do is find some clean clothes., etc.*).

A (10 minutes)

1. Direct students to read the story and underline the time order words.

2. Put students in pairs to discuss their underlined words.

3. Call on volunteers to share their ideas with the class.

> **Activity A Answers, p. 74**
> In the beginning; One day; The next day; After several months; One year later; in the beginning

▶ *Reading and Writing 1, page 75*

B (10 minutes)

1. Read the directions aloud.

2. Direct students to complete the activity individually.

3. Check answers as a class. Have students repeat your pronunciation and intonation of the time order words in the story.

> **Activity B Answers, p. 75**
> **1.** After; **2.** Then; **3.** First; **4.** Next; **5.** later

 For additional practice with time order words, have students visit *Q Online Practice*.

Tip for Success (5 minutes)

1. Have a volunteer read the Tip for Success.

2. Ask students to flip through the student book and find examples of titles that fit this rule.

3. Write a few examples on the board. Explain that many pieces of academic writing have titles and that students can help their grades by remembering this simple capitalization rule.

Q Unit Assignment: Write a story about positive thinking

Unit Question (5 minutes)

Refer students back to the ideas they discussed at the beginning of the unit about positive thinking. Ask students to explain again their answers to the question "What are the benefits of positive thinking?" Cue students if necessary by asking specific questions about the content of the unit: *Are some people positive and other people negative? What are some benefits of positive thinking we discussed? What do you remember from the two readings about positive thinking?* Read the direction lines for the assignment together to ensure understanding.

Learning Outcome

1. Tie the Unit Assignment to the unit learning outcome. Say: *The outcome for this unit is to write about a time when you or someone you know changed a situation with positive thinking. This Unit Assignment is going to let you show your skill in writing a story about positive thinking.*

2. Explain that you are going to use a rubric similar to their Self-Assessment checklist on p. 76 to grade their unit assignments. You can also share a copy of the Unit Assignment Rubric (on p. 42 of this Teacher's Handbook) with the students.

Plan and Write

Brainstorm

A (10 minutes)

1. Direct students to brainstorm with a partner or in a group.

Plan

B (10 minutes)

Tell students to organize their story by writing answers to the questions. Remind them to use verbs in the simple past like *saw* or *went*.

▶ *Reading and Writing 1, page 76*

Write

C (20 minutes)

Have a student volunteer read the directions. Direct students to make a short story using their answers to B. Tell them to look at the story on the top of p. 75 for an example of how to format their paragraph. Before they begin writing, have them look over the checklist on p. 76. Remind them that this will help them to edit their story.

Alternative Unit Assignments

Assign or have students choose one of these assignments to do instead of, or in addition, to the Unit Assignment.

1. Write 3–5 sentences answering this question: Do you believe positive thinking can change a situation? Why or why not?

2. Choose a quote or saying you like from page 62 or one of your own. On a piece of paper, write down the quote or saying. Write several sentences to explain why you like it. Give one example from your life that shows the quote is true for you.

 For an additional unit assignment, have students visit *Q Online Practice.*

Revise and Edit

Peer Review

A (15–20 minutes)

1. Pair students and direct them to read each other's work.

2. Ask students to answer the questions and discuss them.

3. Give students suggestions of helpful feedback: *I liked your writing because… You might try to use more vocabulary words from the unit. The simple past of* find *is* found. *Don't forget to add a title. Check your subject/verb agreement in the third sentence.*

Rewrite

B (15–20 minutes)

Students should review their partners' answers from A and rewrite their paragraphs if necessary.

Edit

C (15–20 minutes)

1. Direct students to read and complete the Self-Assessment checklist. They should be prepared to hand in their work or discuss it in class.

2. Ask for a show of hands for how many students gave all or mostly *Yes* answers.

3. Use the Unit Assignment Rubric on p. 42 in this *Teacher's Handbook* to score each student's assignment.

4. Alternatively, divide the class into large groups and have students read their paragraphs to their group. (Make copies of each student's writing for each person in the group, to assist with scoring.) Pass out copies of the Unit Assignment Rubric and have students grade each other.

▶ *Reading and Writing 1, page 77*

Track Your Success (5 minutes)

1. Have students circle the words they have learned in this unit. Suggest that students go back through the unit to review any words they have forgotten.

2. Have students check the skills they have mastered. If students need more practice to feel confident about their proficiency in a skill, point out the pages numbers and encourage them to review.

3. Read the learning outcome aloud (*Write about a time when you or someone you know changed a situation with positive thinking*). Ask students if they feel that they have met the outcome.

Unit Assignment Rubric

Student name: _____

Date: _____

Unit Assignment: *Write a story about positive thinking.*

20 = Writing element was completely successful (at least 90% of the time).
15 = Writing element was mostly successful (at least 70% of the time).
10 = Writing element was partially successful (at least 50% of the time).
 0 = Writing element was not successful.

Writing a Story	20 points	15 points	10 points	0 points
Story includes a title, has sentences that utilize vocabulary from the unit, and words in sentences are spelled correctly.				
Sentences have both a subject and a verb and those elements agree.				
Story adequately and clearly expresses details about how positive thinking affected a person.				
Simple past tense verbs are used correctly.				
Time order words are used correctly.				

Total points: _____

Comments:

Unit QUESTION
Why is vacation important?

Vacation

READING • reading charts, graphs, and tables
VOCABULARY • compound nouns
WRITING • using correct paragraph structure
GRAMMAR • sentences with *because*

LEARNING OUTCOME

Write a paragraph explaining how much vacation time you need.

▶ *Reading and Writing 1, page 79*
Preview the Unit

Learning Outcome

1. Ask for a volunteer to read the unit skills, then the unit learning outcome (*Write a paragraph explaining how much vacation time you need*).

2. Explain: *This is what you are expected to be able to do by the unit's end. The learning outcome explains how you are going to be evaluated. With this outcome in mind, you should focus on learning these skills (Reading, Vocabulary, Writing, Grammar) that will support your goal of writing a paragraph explaining how much vacation time you need. This can also help you act as mentors in the classroom to help the other students meet this outcome.*

A (10 minutes)

1. Ask students how often your class meets. Ask students to imagine having class every day of the week for many months without a day off. How would they feel?

2. Put students in pairs or small groups to discuss the first two questions.

3. Call on volunteers to share their ideas with the class. Ask questions: *Do you like vacations? Why or why not? What do you like to do during vacation? Where is a popular place for people in your city (or country) to take vacation?*

4. Focus students' attention on the photo. Read the third question aloud. Allow students to call out their ideas and ask them why they think so. Ask about the details of the photo: *Where was this photo taken? Where do you think this man is going? What is he wearing? Why are people around the man in such a hurry?*

Activity A Answers, p. 79
Answers will vary. Possible answers:
1. Schoolchildren have about three months of vacation. Schoolchildren don't have much vacation each year.
2. Teaching gives more vacation time. Police officers get less vacation time. The president of a country gets very little vacation time.
3. The man is wearing a suit. This photo is in the downtown area of a city. The man is going to work. The man is trying to catch a bus. The people are in a hurry.

B (15 minutes)

1. Introduce the Unit Question, *Why is vacation important?* Ask related information questions or questions about personal experience to help students prepare for answering the Unit Question. As they consider the Unit Question, mention jobs like doctors or pilots, for whom vacation is a safety issue. Explain to students that some jobs require vacation breaks so that the workers, such as doctors or pilots, can rest so they won't make mistakes on their jobs. Ask students: *Why do students and teachers need vacation? Why do you need vacation? How does vacation help people do their jobs better? What happens to workers if they never have a vacation? Is there anyone you can think of to whom vacation is not at all important? Why is vacation not important to that person?*

2. Put students in small groups and give each group a piece of poster paper and a marker.

3. Read the Unit Question aloud. Give students a minute to silently consider their answers to the question. Tell students to pass the paper and marker around the group. Direct each group member to write a different answer to the question. Encourage them to help one another.

4. Ask each group to choose a reporter to read the answers to the class. Point out similarities and differences among the answers. If answers from different groups are similar, make a group list that incorporates all of the answers. Post the list to refer to later in the unit.

> **Activity B Answers, p. 79**
> Answers will vary. Possible answers: Vacation is fun. Vacation makes people happy. Vacation helps people be better workers.

The Q Classroom (5 minutes)

CD1, Track 14

1. Play The Q Classroom. Use the example from the audio to help students continue the conversation. Ask: *How did the students answer the question? Do you agree or disagree with their ideas? Why?*

2. On the audio, Marcus says that vacation makes people healthier. Explore this idea further by eliciting things about vacation that makes people healthier (e.g., time with family, laughter, exercise, low stress).

▶ *Reading and Writing 1, page 80*

C (10 minutes)

Ask a volunteer to read the directions aloud. Remind students that the photos are only examples and that they can talk about activities that they like to do that are different from the photos.

> **MULTILEVEL OPTION**
>
> Group lower-level students together and have them simply discuss the activity as described above. Higher-level students should discuss and compare their responses with a partner. Have them find two or three activities that both partners enjoy, and two or three activities that one person likes but the other does not. If time permits, have these students share their answers with the class.

D (10 minutes)

1. Read the directions aloud. Model the activity by reading the first question and answering it aloud. Then point to the box where you would write your response. Ask a student the same question and say: *If X is my partner, I would write his/her answer here*, and point to the box in the *My Partner* column.

2. Elicit answers from volunteers once pairs have completed the activity.

EXPANSION ACTIVITY: Card Swap (10 minutes)

1. Assign each student a number, 1–4. Then ask each student to take out a small slip of paper and write the question from Activity D that corresponds with their numbers. When everyone has their questions written, have the students stand up. (Ensure that the questions are legible.)

2. Explain the rules of the "Card Swap" activity: *When I say, "Go," you'll find a partner. One partner reads his or her question and the second partner answers. Then the second partner asks his or her question, and the first partner answers. Once both partners have answered, they trade slips of paper and look for a new partner. The signal that you are looking for a new partner is that you raise your slip of paper into the air. Continue until I say, "Stop."*

3. You can participate in the activity as well. At the same time, you should ensure that students are circulating around the classroom, finding new partners.

> **MULTILEVEL OPTION**
>
> For this activity, assign some higher-level students the number five. These students can write a fifth question on a slip of paper and ask it during the activity.

READING

▶ *Reading and Writing 1, page 81*

READING 1: Vacation from Work

VOCABULARY (10 minutes)

1. Ask for a volunteer to read the heading and directions aloud. Check students' understanding by asking them what they need to do (read the paragraph and write the bold words next to their corresponding definitions).

2. Check answers as a class. Write each bolded vocabulary word on a separate sheet of paper. Distribute each sheet of paper to one of seven volunteers and ask them to sit/crouch in front of the class.

3. As the class provides a vocabulary word for each blank, have the volunteer who is holding that vocabulary word stand up and repeat the vocabulary word. Ensure that the selected vocabulary item and its pronunciation is correct.

Vocabulary Answers, p. 81
1. stress;   **2.** improve;   **3.** produce;
4. policy;   **5.** employee;   **6.** schedule;
7. reduce

 For additional practice with the vocabulary, have students visit *Q Online Practice*.

Tip for Success (1 minute)

1. Read the Tip for Success.
2. Providing students nouns with their articles (*a girl, an apple,* and *the door*) and verbs using the base infinitive form (*to produce, to improve*) can help students recognize the part of speech for the word when it is viewed out of context (away from its text). Note that this point is covered further in Unit 6.

PREVIEW READING 1 (5 minutes)

1. Read the directions aloud. Ask for a volunteer to remind the class what it means to *scan*. Tell students that they will only have five minutes to find the answers to the preview questions, so they must scan, not read, the email.
2. Tell students they should review their answers after reading.

Preview Reading 1 Answers, p. 81
1. Many employees do not take enough vacation.
2. The email asks employees to decide whether they want to choose vacation policy option 1 or option 2.

Reading 1 Background Note

Some governments around the world have policies in place so that employees of businesses in those countries get vacation time. For example, Finland's government requires businesses to give workers 30 paid days of annual leave a year—as does France's government. Italy, Ireland, Greece, and the United Kingdom require 20 paid days of annual leave a year while Japan and Canada require 10. Many countries, such as Australia, New Zealand, Belgium, and Norway also require employers to offer some paid holidays. Some countries do not require businesses to offer these types of vacation benefits. The United States, for example, has no national policy for paid annual leave or paid holidays—though individual businesses and states may have their own vacation policies.

There are many arguments for countries with no paid annual leave to produce a national policy that requires annual paid time off. Experts note that vacation time allows families to build stronger connections, which is good for society. As well, with more vacation time, families would visit more recreational areas in their own cities and countries—which would increase the amount of money local areas make from tourism. Also, workers who take more vacation are more productive and happier with their jobs.

The argument against paid annual leave is that such a policy is bad for businesses: they would lose money. Experts also say that when employees leave for vacation, those employees who remain on the job feel more stress because of increased workloads.

EXPANSION ACTIVITY: Vacation Policy (10 minutes)

Lead the class in a discussion of your country's vacation policy. What do you know about your country's vacation policy? What do students know about your country's vacation policy? What are some ways to improve your country's vacation policy?

21ST CENTURY SKILLS

In Reading 1, students consider whether a change in vacation policy would be beneficial for a company. In the real world, an important 21st century skill is the ability to analyze and evaluate evidence with the goal of finding a solution to a problem similar to what's done in Reading 1. For example, if employees' productivity levels are dropping, employers often collect and process data in order to develop a lasting solution to the problem.

In the classroom, you can help your students analyze and evaluate evidence regarding a problem by (a) having your students select a problem they see in their community, school, or workplace (b) collecting evidence that they think might be causing that problem, and (c) looking at that evidence to determine what solutions might best fit the problem.

▶ *Reading and Writing 1, page 82*

READ

🔊 CD1, Track 15

1. Instruct sudents to read the email.

2. Play the audio and have students follow along.

▶ *Reading and Writing 1, page 83*

MAIN IDEAS (5 minutes)

1. Ask for a volunteer to read the instructions aloud.

2. Ask students to read and complete the activity individually.

3. Check the answers as a class. Ask students to find the sentence(s) in the email that support their answers.

> **Main Idea Answers, p. 83**
> **1.** Option 1; **2.** Option 2;
> **3.** Option 2; **4.** Option 1

Tip for Success (1 minute)

1. Read the Tip for Success aloud.

2. Prompt students to use this tip with future reading assignments.

DETAILS (10 minutes)

1. Direct students to read the statements and complete the activity.

2. Have students compare answers with a partner.

3. Direct the students to look back at the email to check their answers.

4. Go over the answers with the class.

> **Details Answers, p. 85**
> **1.** Against Change; **2.** Against Change;
> **3.** For Change; **4.** Against Change;
> **5.** For Change; **6.** For Change

 For additional practice with reading comprehension, have students visit *Q Online Practice.*

Learning Outcome

Use the learning outcome to frame the purpose and relevance of Reading 1. Ask: *What did you learn from Reading 1 that prepares you to write a paragraph about how much vacation time you need?*

▶ *Reading and Writing 1, page 85*

Reading Skill: Reading charts, graphs, and tables (5 minutes)

1. Present the information about the reading skill. Have students repeat key vocabulary words like *chart, graph,* and *table.*

2. Check comprehension by asking questions: *Where have you seen charts, graphs, or tables before? Why are they useful? What are some tips for examining charts when you preview a text?*

Skill Note

A common saying is that a picture is worth a thousand words, and with charts, graphs, and tables, that saying is especially true. Charts, graphs, and tables can provide students with a context for the text they are about to read. Scanning the graphic organizers in a text can prepare students for the information that that text will cover, thus helping them process the information more completely and accurately.

To help students practice previewing or scanning charts, graphs, and tables, bring in examples from magazines, books, or newspapers. Ask students to look quickly at the items and decide what kind of information is being shown. Possible answers might be: opinions, stock prices, election results, comparisons between sports teams, etc.

▶ *Reading and Writing 1, page 86*

A (10 minutes)

Direct students to read the table, questions and complete the activity. Have students check their answers with a partner before you go over them as a class.

> **Reading Skill A Answers, p. 86**
> **1.** Vacations and Holidays Around the World;
> **2.** Countries, Vacation Days, Holidays, Total Days Off;
> **3.** Answers will vary. Possible answer: Vacation Policy;
> **4.** Finland;
> **5.** France, Germany, United States;
> **6.** 19;
> **7.** 21;
> **8.** Vietnam

Critical Thinking Tip (3 minutes)

1. Read the Critical Thinking Tip aloud.

2. Encourage students to use charts, graphs, and tables at school or in the workplace to help others easily understand what they want to say.

Critical Q: Expansion Activity

Interpreting Tables or Graphs

1. Divide the class into three groups, and provide each with a written scenario that can be illustrated with a chart, table, or graph. Groups should not know each others' scenarios.
Examples: 1) 45% of students think classes should be longer; 65% of students think classes should be shorter. 2) Nine companies refuse to offer paid vacation; 18 companies want to offer paid vacation but cannot because of budget concerns; 51 companies offer paid vacation. 3) More cities are requiring businesses to offer paid holiday leave in 2010 than they did in 1990.

2. When each group has a scenario, have each group create a chart, table, or graph that represents its scenario.

3. Have each group present its graphic organizer to the class. The audience can give feedback on how clearly the organizer presents its information.

▶ *Reading and Writing 1, page 87*

B (10 minutes)

1. Read the directions aloud. Direct students to answer the questions individually based on the bar graph.

2. Check answers as a class.

> **Reading Skill B Answers, p. 87**
> 1. Reasons Employees Do Not Take Vacation;
> 2. It's too expensive;
> 3. One person;
> 4. 40 people

 For additional practice with reading charts, graphs, and tables, have students visit *Q Online Practice*.

WHAT DO YOU THINK? (20 minutes)

1. Ask students to read the questions and reflect on their answers.

2. Seat students in small groups and assign roles: a group leader to make sure everyone contributes, a note-taker to record the group's ideas, a reporter to share the group's ideas with the class, and a timekeeper to watch the clock.

3. Give students five minutes to discuss the questions. Call time if conversations are winding down. Allow them an extra minute or two if necessary.

4. Call on each group's reporter to share ideas with the class.

5. Have each student choose one of the questions and write two or three sentences in response.

6. Call on volunteers to share ideas with the class.

> **MULTILEVEL OPTION**
>
> Have lower-level students count the students in their group who are for and who are against the change. Have them share the result with the class.
> Have higher-level students create a chart or graph using the data the lower-level students just collected. Alternatively, have higher-level students propose a change or addition to their school's or work's vacation policy.

> **What Do You Think? Answers, p. 87**
> Answers will vary. Possible answers:
> 1. I am against the change because vacation is too expensive for employees. I am for the change because workers check their email on vacation.
> 2. At my school, teachers get vacation each summer. At my job, we don't get vacation because the boss would lose money.

▶ *Reading and Writing 1, page 88*

READING 2: Vacation from School

VOCABULARY (15 minutes)

1. Direct students to read the words and definitions in the box. Model pronunciation and have students repeat the words.

2. Have students work with a partner to complete the sentences. Call on volunteers to read the completed sentences aloud.

3. Have the pairs create one new sentence for each vocabulary item.

4. Select model sentences and ask students to write them on the board. Practice group editing if necessary using items 2–5 from the rubric on page 98.

> **Vocabulary Answers, p. 88**
> 1. relax; 2. compete; 3. experience; 4. review;
> 5. average; 6. bored; 7. discover

 For additional practice with the vocabulary, have students visit *Q Online Practice*.

PREVIEW READING 2 (10 minutes)

1. Ask for a volunteer to read the directions. Ask for a different volunteer to refresh the class's memory about skimming. Direct students to skim the letters and answer the questions.

2. Tell students they should review their answers after reading.

> **Preview Reading 2 Answers, p. 89**
> **1.** James Walsh; **2.** Linda Smith

Reading 2 Background Note

Letters to the editor, in newspapers and magazines, are often the best place to find out what people in your area are thinking and feeling on particular topics. Not everyone likes to write letters, but those who do, and those whom newspaper editors select, tend to represent a broad array of local and national opinions. Historians often look at old periodicals (e.g., newspapers and magazines) to understand what "average" people felt about the important issues of the day. Often, history remembers the most important people, and "average" voices are not remembered. Letters to the editor provide one important way for "average" voices to be heard and recorded in the historical record.

READND

▶)) CD1, Track 16

1. Instruct students to read the letters.

2. Play the audio and have students follow along.

MAIN IDEAS (5 minutes)

1. Read the directions aloud.

2. Ask students to read and complete the activity individually.

3. Ask for volunteers to share their answers. Check students' understanding of the main ideas by asking: *Which letter writer supports long summer vacations? Why was the person for a long school vacation? Why was the other person against it?*

> **Main Idea Answers, p. 90**
> **1.** James Walsh; **2.** Linda Smith; **3.** James Walsh;
> **4.** Linda Smith

DETAILS (15 minutes)

A (5 minutes)

1. Direct students to read the statements and complete the activity.

2. Have students compare answers with a partner.

3. Direct the students to look back at the letters to check their answers.

4. Go over the answers with the class.

> **Activity A Answers, p. 91**
> **1.** a; **2.** c; **3.** b; **4.** a

B (10 minutes)

1. Direct students to read the questions and complete the activity.

2. Have students compare answers with a partner.

3. Direct students to look back at the bar graph to check their answers.

4. Go over the answers with the class.

> **Activity B Answers, p. 91**
> **1.** 191; **2.** 185; **3.** 200; **4.** Japan;
> **5.** South Korea; **6.** United States

 For additional practice with reading comprehension, have students visit *Q Online Practice*.

WHAT DO YOU THINK?

A (10 minutes)

1. Ask students to read the questions and reflect on their answers.

2. Seat students in small groups and assign roles: a group leader to make sure everyone contributes, a note-taker to record the group's ideas, a reporter to share the group's ideas with the class, and a timekeeper to watch the clock.

3. Give students five minutes to discuss the questions. Call time if conversations are winding down. Allow them an extra minute or two if necessary.

> **Activity A Answers, p. 92**
> Answers will vary. Possible answers:
> **1.** I had two months of vacation from school. I had summers off. I think it was enough time.
> **2.** I went to the beach on vacation. I worked with my family. I read books. I learned to work with my father during vacation. I learned how to swim.

B (15 minutes)

1. Tell the students that they should think about both Reading 1 and Reading 2 as they answer the questions in B. After a brief discussion with their group, students will choose one of the questions and write three or four sentences in response.

2. Ask students to read their sentences with a partner.

3. Call on each pair to share ideas with the class.

> **Activity B Answers, p. 92**
> Answers will vary. Possible answers:
> **1.** Long summer vacations are necessary because children need a break. Long summer vacations are not necessary because they will forget what they have learned.
> **2.** Children need more vacation time than adults because they need time to play. Adults need more vacation time than children because they work harder.

Learning Outcome

Use the learning outcome to frame the purpose and relevance of Readings 1 and 2 and the Critical Q activity. Ask: *What did you learn from Reading 2 that prepares you to write a paragraph explaining how much vacation time you need? What did you learn from the Critical Q Expansion Activity that will help you write a paragraph explaining how much vacation time you need?*

Vocabulary Skill:
Compound nouns (5 minutes)

1. Ask for volunteers to read about compound nouns.

2. Check comprehension: *What is a compound noun? Can you think of examples of compound nouns?* (Some examples: *toothpaste, swimming pool,* and *health center.*) *Why is it useful to learn about compound nouns?*

Skill Note

Compound nouns can be quite difficult for beginning-level students to recognize and use properly. The reason for the difficulty is that students, just learning what nouns are and how they function, now have to think of some nouns as adjectives. One way to present this challenge to students is by continuing to help them recognize nouns. When they find two

nouns in a row (one directly following another), that is often a clue that students have found a compound noun—where the first noun is modifying (or acting as an adjective for) the second noun.

To practice this, present students with several example sentences with compound nouns. **Examples:** *I wanted to go to the computer store today. It is impossible that they lost your voter registration form in the mail.* Ask students to find the places where they see two (or more) nouns in a row. Those instances are examples of compound nouns. Have students continue to hone this skill in the coming activities.

A (5 minutes)

1. Read the directions aloud. Go over the first phrase together as an example. Direct students to work independently. Walk around to check that students are on the right track.

2. Go over the answers with the class.

> **Activity A Answers, pp. 92–93**
> **1.** life experience;   **2.** work experience;
> **3.** relaxation time;   **4.** work time;
> **5.** job stress;   **6.** family stress;
> **7.** school program;   **8.** math program;
> **9.** summer activity;   **10.** school activities;
> **11.** school rules;   **12.** vacation rules

▶ *Reading and Writing 1, page 93*

B (10 minutes)

Ask for a volunteer to read the directions aloud. Go over the first sentence together. Direct students to work independently.

> **Activity B Answers, p. 93**
> **1.** What is your school schedule?
> **2.** How long is your school year?
> **3.** Which is your favorite summer month?
> **4.** What do you do on your summer vacation?
> **5.** What kind of work experience do you have?
> **6.** What kind of life experiences do teenagers need?

 For additional practice with compound nouns, have students visit *Q Online Practice.*

C (10 minutes)

Have students compare their answers with a partner and practice asking and answering the questions. Make this a mixed-ability activity.

WRITING

▶ *Reading and Writing 1, page 94*

Writing Skill: Using correct paragraph structure (15 minutes)

1. Pass out a few examples of paragraphs to the students that you photocopied before class. Take them from the textbook or other sources.

2. Explain the idea of *topic, supporting,* and *concluding sentences* from the writing skill. Ask volunteers to read the definition of each.

3. Check comprehension: *What is a paragraph? What are the three kinds of sentences a paragraph usually has? What does a supporting sentence do? What does it mean to indent?*

4. Review the photocopied example paragraphs with the students. Have them label the *topic, supporting,* and *concluding sentences.* Use the activity from the following Skill Note to increase students' familiarity with these different types of sentences in a paragraph.

Skill Note

Academic writing requires students to group ideas into paragraphs. Sometimes those ideas need long paragraphs, and sometimes those ideas need short paragraphs. However, each paragraph needs to focus on a single idea. The earlier students can recognize the form and function of paragraphs, the easier their future writings will be.

To help students recognize the form of paragraphs, give students a text that includes paragraphs and ask them to count how many paragraphs they see. Next, elicit clues from students as to how they could tell each block of text was a paragraph (e.g., indentation or many sentences in one group). Then have them choose one paragraph and look for the three paragraph parts listed in the lesson.

A (5 minutes)

Read the directions aloud. Direct students to underline and label the sentences to complete the activity. Have them check their answers with a partner.

Activity A Answers, p. 94

TS: Vacations are not the right answer to worker stress.
SS: First of all, one or two vacations a year cannot reduce the stress of many days of long work hours. Also, vacations can actually be very stressful because they are expensive and difficult. Finally, people lived for thousands of years without vacations.
CS: Vacations are not necessary.

▶ *Reading and Writing 1, page 95*

B (10 minutes)

1. Ask for a volunteer to read the directions aloud. Remind students that they should use each number only once.

2. Check the answers as a class. Ask students to support their answers with evidence from the previous activity on paragraphs.

Activity B Answers, p. 95

Order of sentences: 4, 2, 5, 1, and 3

 For additional practice with using correct paragraph structure, have students visit *Q Online Practice.*

C (5 minutes)

Review as a class what students have to do. This activity could be done in class or assigned as homework.

Grammar: Sentences with *because* (5 minutes)

1. Read the presentation aloud. Ask for volunteers to read the sample sentences.

2. Elicit examples from students of times when they use the word *because.* Write a few of their examples on the board. Use the following Skill Note to explain how their examples can be examples of *cause* and *effect.*

3. Check comprehension by asking questions: *When do we use* because *to combine two sentences? What does it say about using a comma with* because*? Why do we use a pronoun in the sentence about Lucy rather than repeating her name two times?*

Skill Note

Because is a word that creates adverbial clauses of *cause* for a particular effect. For example, in the sentence *He is coming to the office because the computers don't work, He is coming to the office* is the effect caused by *because the computers don't work.*

Sometimes, English speakers use the *because* adverbial clause by itself (e.g., *Why are you in a hurry? **Because I am late.***) However, such use creates an incomplete sentence because that adverbial clause *depends on* the "effect" part of the sentence to create a complete sentence.

▶ *Reading and Writing 1, page 96*

A (10 minutes)

1. Read the example together. Point out the use of the comma in the second sentence. Direct students to write sentences using *because*.

2. Put students in pairs to discuss their answers.

3. Call on volunteers to share their ideas with the class.

> **Activity A Answers, p. 96**
> **1.** a. People take vacations because they need a break from work. b. Because people need a break from work, they take vacations;
> **2.** a. Truck drivers have a lot of job stress because they work long hours. b. Because truck drivers work long hours, they have a lot of job stress;
> **3.** a. Some employees don't take vacations because they don't have paid vacation. b. Because some employees don't have paid vacation, they don't take vacations;
> **4.** a. Some employees have special schedules because they have family needs. b. Because some employees have family needs, they have special schedules;.
> **5.** a. Children don't learn about the world because they spend all their time in school. b. Because children spend all their time in school, they don't learn about the world.

B (5 minutes)

1. Tell students to read the directions silently and write their answers. When finished, they should read their sentences to a partner and listen to their partner's sentences.

> **Activity B Answers, p. 96**
> Answers will vary. Possible answers:
> **1.** I like to go on vacation in the summer because I am able to visit new places.
> **2.** Today, people have a lot of work stress because they work too many hours.

 For additional practice with sentences with *because,* have students visit *Q Online Practice.*

▶ *Reading and Writing 1, page 97*

Unit Assignment:
Write a paragraph giving reasons

Unit Question (5 minutes)

Refer students back to the ideas they discussed at the beginning of the unit about vacation. Remind students about their answers to the questions on page 79. Cue students if necessary by asking specific questions about the content of the unit: *Do you remember the two letters we read about vacation time? What were some reasons why people need to take a vacation? In the charts we looked at, which countries require the most paid annual leave (vacation + holidays)? Why are such vacations important?* Read the direction lines for the assignment together to ensure understanding.

Learning Outcome

1. Tie the Unit Assignment to the unit learning outcome. Say: *The outcome for this unit is to write a paragraph explaining how much vacation time you need. This Unit Assignment is going to let you show your skill in writing a paragraph and writing sentences with* because.

2. Explain that you are going to use a rubric similar to their Self-Assessment checklist on p. 98 to grade their Unit Assignment. You can also share a copy of the Unit Assignment Rubric (on p. 53 of this *Teacher's Handbook*) with the students.

Plan and Write

Brainstorm

A (10 minutes)

1. Read the directions aloud. Direct students to discuss the questions with a partner to complete the activity.

Plan

B (10 minutes)

Ask students to read the directions silently. Direct students to choose the best reasons from Activity A and write their ideas.

Tip for Success (1 minute)

1. Read the Tip for Success aloud.

2. Introductory phrases provide a context for the sentence (e.g., *in the morning* tells the reader that the sentence will take place in the context of the morning; *First of all* tells the reader that the sentence will talk about the first of several topics, reasons). When a piece of information begins a sentence *and* provides a context, there should be a comma after that phrase.

Write

C (15 minutes)

1. Read the directions aloud. Tell students to look at the checklist on p. 98 to guide their writing.

Alternative Unit Assignments

Assign or have students choose one of these assignments to do instead of, or in addition to, the Unit Assignment.

1. Imagine that you are the owner of a busy restaurant. What are the vacation rules for your employees? Are the rules the same for everyone, or are there different rules for different types of employees? Write down the vacation rules for the restaurant. Explain why you decided on them.

2. Your school or workplace wants to reduce the vacation time. Write a letter to your editor. Do you think less vacation is a good idea? Why or why not? Write your reasons in the letter.

 For an additional unit assignment, have students visit *Q Online Practice*.

▶ *Reading and Writing 1, page 98*
Revise and Edit

Peer Review

A (15–20 minutes)

1. Pair students and direct them to read each other's work.

2. Ask students to answer the questions and discuss them.

3. Give students suggestions of helpful feedback: *Your concluding sentence was very strong. You should put your topic sentence before your supporting sentences. Paragraphs need to be indented. There is a problem with subject–verb agreement in the second sentence.*

Rewrite

B (15–20 minutes)

Students should review their partners' answers from A and rewrite their paragraphs if necessary.

Edit

C (15–20 minutes)

1. Direct students to read and complete the Self-Assessment checklist. They should be prepared to hand in their work or discuss it in class.

2. Ask for a show of hands for how many students gave all or mostly *Yes* answers.

3. Use the Unit Assignment Rubric on p. 53 in this *Teacher's Handbook* to score each student's assignment.

4. Alternatively, divide the class into large groups and have students read their paragraphs to their group. (Make copies of each student's writing for each person in the group, to assist with scoring.) Pass out copies of the Unit Assignment Rubric and have students grade each other.

▶ *Reading and Writing 1, page 99*
Track Your Success (5 minutes)

1. Have students circle the words they have learned in this unit. Suggest that students go back through the unit to review any words they have forgotten.

2. Have students check the skills they have mastered. If students need more practice to feel confident about their proficiency in a skill, point out the pages numbers and encourage them to review.

3. Read the learning outcome aloud (*Write a paragraph explaining how much vacation time you need*). Ask students if they feel that they have met the outcome.

Unit Assignment Rubric

Student name: _____

Date: _____

Unit Assignment: *Write a paragraph giving reasons.*

20 = Writing element was completely successful (at least 90% of the time).
15 = Writing element was mostly successful (at least 70% of the time).
10 = Writing element was partially successful (at least 50% of the time).
 0 = Writing element was not successful.

Writing a Paragraph	20 points	15 points	10 points	0 points
Paragraph uses vocabulary from the unit and words in the paragraph are spelled correctly.				
Sentences with *because* are correct.				
Sentences have both a subject and a verb and those elements agree.				
Paragraph structure is correct and the first line of every paragraph is indented.				
Reasons for vacation time and how much time is necessary are clear and specific.				

Total points: _____

Comments:

Unit QUESTION

What makes you laugh?

Laughter

READING • identifying the topic sentence in a paragraph
VOCABULARY • using the dictionary
GRAMMAR • sentences with *when*
WRITING • writing a topic sentence

LEARNING OUTCOME

Explain what makes you or someone you know laugh.

▶ *Reading and Writing 1, page 101*

Preview the Unit

Learning Outcome

1. Ask for a volunteer to read the unit skills, then the unit learning outcome.

2. Explain: *This is what you are expected to be able to do by the unit's end. The learning outcome explains how you are going to be evaluated. With this outcome in mind, you should focus on learning these skills (Reading, Vocabulary, Writing, Grammar) that will support your goal of explaining what makes you laugh. This can also help you act as mentors in the classroom to help the other students meet this outcome.*

A (10 minutes)

1. Elicit from students times when they laugh. Have students write on the board the situations in which they laugh (e.g., movies, jokes with friends).

2. Put students in pairs or small groups to discuss the first two questions.

3. Call on volunteers to share their ideas with the class. Ask questions: *When was the last time you laughed? How would you describe that laugh? Why is it important to laugh?*

4. Focus students' attention on the photo. Have a volunteer describe the photo to the class. Read the third question aloud. Ask: *How do you imagine these women's laughs sound? Who appears to be laughing more? Would you also laugh if you were in the same situation as the women in the photo?*

Activity A Answers, p. 101
Answers will vary. Possible answers:
1. Yes, I laugh often. No, I do not laugh often.
2. I have a loud laugh. I have a quiet laugh. I don't know what kind of laugh I have.
3. They're laughing because the birds are so close to them/flying in their faces. They're laughing at the birds. The woman on the right looks like she's laughing because she is surprised. They're laughing because the birds are tickling them.

B (10 minutes)

1. Introduce the Unit Question, *What makes you laugh?* Ask related information questions or questions about personal experience to help students prepare for answering the Unit Question. Ask about movies they've seen, jokes they've heard, or fun activities they've done to get them thinking about what they find funny.

2. Read the Unit Question aloud. Point out that answers to the questions can fall into categories (e.g., jokes, movies, stories, pictures, other). Give students a minute to silently consider their answers to the question and categories the class can use.

3. Write each category at the top of a sheet of poster paper. Elicit responses to the Unit Question from students that fall into these categories. Make notes under the correct heading.

4. Post the lists to refer to later in the unit.

Activity B Answers, p. 101
Answers will vary. Possible answers: My friends make me laugh. I laugh at TV shows. Jokes people make about me make me laugh.

The Q Classroom (5 minutes)

CD2, Track 02

1. Play The Q Classroom. Use the example from the audio to help students continue the conversation. Ask: *How did the students answer the question? Do you agree or disagree with their ideas? Why?*

2. Say: *In the audio, the students talk about many things that make them laugh. Sophy says that funny TV shows make her laugh. Marcus says he laughs when he hears comedians. Felix and Yuna have their own ideas as well.* Ask: *Which student in this audio are you most like? Do you laugh at the things Marcus laughs at? Or Yuna? The other students? Why or why not?*

▶ *Reading and Writing 1, page 102*

C (10 minutes)

1. Ask for a volunteer to read the directions aloud. Check students' understanding by asking what they need to do to complete the activity (look at the photos, write why they think the person is laughing, and discuss in a group).

2. Circulate and provide help with vocabulary as needed.

D (5 minutes)

1. Tell students that now that they have discussed the photos, they should talk about their own experiences. Read the directions aloud and direct students to complete the activity in their groups.

EXPANSION ACTIVITY: Joke Telephone (10 minutes)

1. Explain that one of the traditions surrounding laughter is joke telling. Ask: *Are jokes an important tradition in your culture?*

2. Divide students into three or four groups and line them up. Have the first person in each line nearest the board, and make sure the other members line up behind the first person, leaving a few feet of space between each member of the group.

3. Write out three or four jokes on four pieces of paper. Three example jokes: (1) Why did the boy bring a ladder to school? He wanted to go to high school. (2) A man arrived on Friday in a small town. He stayed for two days and left on Friday. How is this possible? His horse's name is Friday! (3) Why is six afraid of seven? Because seven ate nine.

4. Give one slip of paper to each student in the back of each line. This student reads the joke and then whispers it to the student in from of him or her. Next, that student whispers it to the student in front of them. The joke is passed up the line, with one student telling another, until it gets to the first person in line. The first person in line writes the joke on the board.

5. If the joke has changed (lost or gained words) as it was passed up the line, the student with the slip of paper at the back of the line should make corrections.

6. Together, the class should try to figure out what makes the jokes funny.

READING

▶ *Reading and Writing 1, page 103*

READING 1: What is Laughter?

VOCABULARY (10 minutes)

1. Ask for a volunteer to read the directions aloud. Direct students to match the bold words with their definitions.

2. Have students check answers with a partner. Then check answers as a class.

MULTILEVEL OPTION

Allow lower-level students to work in groups to complete the matching activity. Higher-level students should complete the activity independently and then write a short paragraph using three or four of the bold words.

Alternatively, place students in mixed-ability pairs. The higher-level students can assist lower-level students in filling in the blanks and explain their understanding of the meaning of the words. Direct students to alternate reading the sentences aloud. Encourage them to help each other with pronunciation.

Vocabulary Answers, p. 103
a. nervous;   **b.** protect;   **c.** joke;
d. natural;   **e.** embarrassed;   **f.** honest;
g. pretend;   **h.** surprise

 For additional practice with the vocabulary, have students visit *Q Online Practice.*

Tip for Success (1 minute)

1. Read the Tip for Success with students.

2. Tell students this is a great rule to begin forming adjectives from verbs. However, they should keep in mind that adjectives are actually formed from the participle form of the verb. Thus, the adjective form of *to write*, for example, is *written* not *wrote*.

PREVIEW READING 1 (5 minutes)

1. Remind them what they've learned about skimming and scanning in previous units. Direct them to answer the preview questions to complete the activity.

2. Tell students they should review their answers after reading.

> **Preview Reading 1 Answers, p. 103**
> What is laughter? When do people laugh? What is funny? Why doesn't everyone laugh at the same joke?

Reading 1 Background Note

Scientific research shows that there are four areas in which laughter positively affects someone's health.

1. Laughter helps a person relax his or her body. When a person laughs, stress and tension leaves his or her muscles.

2. Laughter helps the body fight off diseases and infections.

3. Laughter helps a person's heart by increasing blood flow and reducing the risk of heart attacks.

4. Laughter makes people feel good and can even relieve some pain.

21ST CENTURY SKILLS

In our ever-increasing globalized world, colleagues work together across cultural boundaries. When "breaking the ice" with new colleagues, humor is an oft-used tool. However, humor does not always translate well, and something that one person thinks is funny can be seen by another person as rude. That is definitely not the way to start a professional relationship!

It's important to know when it is OK to tell jokes in different situations. Have your students think about when it is OK to tell a joke. Ask: *Is it too soon to tell a joke when you are starting a conversation? Is humor a good way to start a conversation? When is it not OK to tell jokes? When is the right time to tell jokes?* Say: *Perhaps someone you don't know well would not like some jokes you find funny, whereas a story or act of kindness or politeness would be more appropriate.*

▶ *Reading and Writing 1, page 104*

READ

◉ CD2, Track 03

1. Instruct students to read the article.

2. Play the audio and have students follow along.

▶ *Reading and Writing 1, page 105*

MAIN IDEAS (5 minutes)

1. Ask students to read and complete the activity individually.

2. Ask for volunteers to share their answers and direct students to point to the place in the article where they found each answer.

> **Main Idea Answers, p. 105**
> **1.** b; **2.** b; **3.** b; **4.** a

DETAILS (5 minutes)

1. Direct students to read the statements and complete the activity.

2. Have students compare answers with a partner.

3. Direct the students to look back at the article to check their answers.

4. Go over the answers with the class.

> **Details Answers, p. 105**
> **1.** F; **2.** T; **3.** F; **4.** T; **5.** T; **6.** F

 For additional practice with reading comprehension, have students visit *Q Online Practice*.

▶ *Reading and Writing 1, page 106*

WHAT DO YOU THINK? (10 minutes)

1. Ask students to read the questions and reflect on and check their answers.

2. Seat students in pairs.

3. Give students five minutes to complete the chart and discuss the chart and questions. Call time if conversations are winding down. Allow them an extra minute or two if necessary.

4. Call on each group's reporter to share ideas with the class.

5. Have each student choose one of the questions and write 2–3 sentences in response.

6. Call on volunteers to share ideas with the class.

What Do You Think? Answers, p. 106
Answers will vary.

MULTILEVEL OPTION

Have lower-level students write fewer sentences. Have higher-level students write more by expanding upon their answers with specific details.

Learning Outcome

Use the learning outcome to frame the purpose and relevance of Reading 1. Ask: *What did you learn from Reading 1 that prepares you to explain what makes you or someone you know laugh? What did you learn that will help you with this explanation?*

Reading Skill: Identifying the topic sentence in a paragraph (5 minutes)

1. Ask for volunteers to each read aloud one of the sentences of the explanation, then have students read the paragraph silently. Remind students that a paragraph should only contain one idea, and thus one topic sentence.

2. Check comprehension by asking questions: *What is a topic sentence? Is the topic sentence always first? How did you know that the bold sentence in the example was the topic sentence?*

Skill Note

In order to write good topic sentences, and know where to place them within paragraphs, students have to know how to recognize topic sentences. Show the class some examples to model what topic sentences look like and how they fit into the paragraphs. To practice this skill, have them turn to the first paragraph of some of the readings from previous units of this textbook and search for topic sentences. This could be done now or after completing Activities A and B.

▶ *Reading and Writing 1, page 107*

A (10 minutes)

1. Direct students to read and follow the directions to complete the activity. Tell students to check their answers with a partner when they finish.

2. When everyone is finished, check answers as a class and see if there are any questions.

Reading Skill A Answers, p. 107
1. People can learn to laugh.
2. People laugh more when they speak than when they listen.

B (5 minutes)

1. Read the directions aloud. Ask students to confirm their understanding of the activity by telling you what they need to do.

2. When students finish, check answers as a class.

Reading Skill B Answers, p. 107
1. Laughter is natural for people.
2. Laughter connects us with other people.
3. It is difficult to pretend to laugh.
4. Most laughter is about being friendly with other people.
5. We often laugh when we feel nervous.
6. Sometimes we laugh because we think we are better than other people.
7. Some things are funny because we don't expect them.
8. Silly things are sometimes funny.
9. Not everyone has the same sense of humor.
10. Our idea of what is funny changes with time.

 For additional practice with identifying the topic sentence in a paragraph, have students visit *Q Online Practice*.

READING 2: The Best Medicine Is Laughter

VOCABULARY (10 minutes)

1. Write the bolded vocabulary on the board and probe for prior knowledge. *What words do you already know? What do those words mean?* When writing nouns on board, use articles (*a, an, the*) when appropriate. When writing verbs, use the infinitive form. Using articles and infinitive forms can help students differentiate nouns and verbs, especially when the words are the same (e.g. *a cry* vs. *to cry*).

2. Put students in pairs or groups of three. Have groups read sentences 1–8 and try to match each with definitions a–h. Encourage students to make guesses and emphasize that it's OK to be wrong.

3. Ask different volunteers to read sentences 1–8 in turn.

4. Ask students to vote on which definition best matches the given sentence and tally answers on the board. Provide or confirm correct answers.

> **Vocabulary Answers, pp. 107–108**
> **a.** effect;   **b.** prevent;   **c.** pain;   **d.** rate;
> **e.** breathe;   **f.** increase;   **g.** fear;   **h.** cry

 For additional practice with the vocabulary, have students visit *Q Online Practice.*

MULTILEVEL OPTION

Group lower-level students and assist them with the task. Provide alternate example sentences to help them understand the words. Here are some example sentences for possibly tricky vocabulary. *Beets grow at a faster **rate** than potatoes. My heart **rate** increases when I laugh. The **effect** of laughing is that people feel healthy. The best **effect** is that your heart gets stronger.*

Have higher-level students complete the activity individually and then compare answers with a partner. Tell the pairs to write an additional sample sentence for each vocabulary item. Have volunteers write one of their sentences on the board. Correct the sentences with the whole class as needed, focusing on the use of the given vocabulary item rather than other grammatical issues.

Tip for Success (1 minute)

1. Read the Tip for Success.

2. Remind students to continue to add one new word a day to their student dictionaries.

▶ *Reading and Writing 1, page 108*

PREVIEW READING 2 (10 minutes)

Have students complete the task individually. Check as a class.

> **Preview Reading 2 Answer, p. 108**
> **1.** Practice laughing

Reading 2 Background Note

A group of laughter clubs was founded by Dr. Madan Kataria, an Indian physician, in 1995. They were begun to encourage people to come together and enjoy the health benefits of laughing. Eventually, laughter clubs were paired with yoga and laughter yoga was born. In these clubs, participants mix yoga positions with laughter, seeking to gain the health benefits of both actions. Practitioners of laughter yoga believe that even fake laughter can benefit a person's health—even if people don't really enjoy the sound of fake laughter. One can now find laughter yoga seminars in schools and business environments. Laughter is truly a strong medicine!

READUD

🔊 CD2, Track 04

1. Instruct students to read the article.

2. Play the audio and have students follow along.

▶ *Reading and Writing 1, page 110*

MAIN IDEAS (5 minutes)

1. Read the directions aloud.

2. Ask students to read and complete the activity individually.

3. You can check students' answers visually by asking them to hold up the number of fingers that corresponds to their answer (if they answered "7" for the first item they should hold up seven fingers). If there appear to be several students with the wrong answers, stop and discuss.

> **Main Idea Answers, p. 110**
> **a.** 7;   **b.** 4;   **c.** 2;   **d.** 6;   **e.** 3;   **f.** 1;   **g.** 5

DETAILS (5 minutes)

1. Direct students to read the statements and complete the activity.

2. Have students compare answers with a partner.

3. Direct the students to look back at the article to check their answers.

4. Go over the answers with the class.

Details Answers, p. 110
1. F; **2.** T; **3.** T; **4.** F; **5.** T; **6.** F

 For additional practice with reading comprehension, have students visit *Q Online Practice*.

WHAT DO YOU THINK?

A (10 minutes)

1. Ask students to read the questions and reflect on their answers.

2. Seat students in small groups and assign roles: a group leader to make sure everyone contributes, a note-taker to record the group's ideas, a reporter to share the group's ideas with the class, and, if there are enough students, a timekeeper to watch the clock.

3. Give students five minutes to discuss the questions. Call time if conversations are winding down. Allow them an extra minute or two if necessary.

Activity A Answers, pp. 110–111
1. Answers will vary. Possible answers: When I laugh, I breathe quickly. After I laugh, my stomach hurts. Laughing makes my heart rate increase.
2. Answers will vary.

▶ *Reading and Writing 1, page 111*

B (5 minutes)

1. Tell the students that they should think about both Reading 1 and Reading 2 as they answer the questions in B. Students will choose one of the questions and write three or four sentences in response.

2. Ask students to read their sentences with a partner.

3. Call on each pair to share ideas with the class.

Activity B Answers, p. 111
Answers will vary. Possible answers:
1. Watching funny TV shows can make me laugh more. Telling and listening to jokes can get more laughter in my life. Maybe I'll join a laughter club.

2. It is important for a person to have a sense of humor because they will laugh more and be healthier. It is not important for a person to have a sense of humor because laughter is not the only thing that can make people healthy.

MULTILEVEL OPTION

Pair lower-level students with higher-level students. Have the higher-level students tell classroom-appropriate jokes to try to get the lower-level students to laugh. Be sure to have them preview the jokes with you first to check for language level and appropriateness.

Learning Outcome

Use the learning outcome to frame the purpose and relevance of Readings 1 and 2. Ask: *What did you learn from Reading 2 that prepares you to explain what makes you or someone you know laugh? What did you learn that will help you with this explanation?*

Vocabulary Skill: Using the dictionary
(15 minutes)

1. Have volunteers read the presentation material aloud, two sentences each.

2. Incorporate the following Skill Note into the presentation of this vocabulary skill. Tell students that dictionaries are very useful for finding how words are used in different parts of speech (e.g., *to laugh* (v.) and *laughter* (n.)).

3. Select two of three vocabulary words from this unit, such as *honest, joke,* and *breathe,* and lead students through the activity in the Skill Note.

4. After they complete the activity, check comprehension: *What are some examples of parts of speech? Why is it helpful to know the parts of speech? What are the different parts of speech for joke? Can anyone use them in a sentence? What is the abbreviation for noun? What is the abbreviation for adjective?*

Skill Note

Differentiating between parts of speech can be difficult for new English language learners to do. English contains many words that look nearly identical yet function as different parts of speech (e.g., *milk* (n.), *to milk* (v.), *milky* (adj.)). Dictionaries are one tool that students have that can help them understand the different uses of these similar words in their different roles in the sentence.

Help students differentiate between different parts of speech by having students look up the vocabulary items from this unit in their dictionaries. Ask students to note all the different parts of speech these words' listings include. If possible, have them use learner's dictionaries, since they often provide sentences showing the context for each word.

▶ *Reading and Writing 1, page 112*

A (10 minutes)

1. Have students to read the directions silently. Check that there are enough dictionaries for the second part of the activity.

2. Go over the answers with the class.

> **Activity A Answers, p. 112**
> **1.** adjective; **2.** noun; **3.** verb; **4.** verb;
> **5.** noun; **6.** verb; **7.** adjective; **8.** adverb

B (10 minutes)

Ask for a volunteer to read the directions aloud. Do the first sentence together as an example. Ask students to check their answers with a partner before going over the answers as a class.

> **Activity B Answers, p. 112**
> **1.** embarrassed; **2.** introduce; **3.** nature;
> **4.** breathe; **5.** prevent; **6.** anger

 For additional practice with using a dictionary, have students visit *Q Online Practice*.

Tip for Success (1 minute)

Read the Tip for Success. When presenting new vocabulary items to students, presenting them in context (i.e., in a sentence or a group of sentences) can provide crucial clues that will help students determine a word's definition, part of speech, and collocations.

▶ *Reading and Writing 1, page 113*

Grammar: Sentences with *when*
(10 minutes)

1. Ask for a volunteer to read aloud the first paragraph. Continue presenting the rest of the information to the students. Ask: *Why do you use* when *in sentences? Do you ever use commas when you begin a sentence with* when? Explain: *Commas can help your reader understand where one idea stops and another related idea starts.*

2. Practice using *when* adverbial clauses by leading students through the activity explained in the following Skill Note. Correct sentences as a class and point out which part of the sentences are "situations" and which are "actions." Point out how *when* combines the two ideas, and draw special attention to comma usage.

3. Check comprehension: *When can you combine two sentences using* when? *When do sentences with* when *need a comma? Can you give another example? When do sentences with* when *not need a comma? Can you give another example?*

Skill Note

When is a word that creates adverbial clauses that introduce a situation. For example, in the sentence *When he comes to the office, he'll fix the computers, When he comes to the office* introduces the situation where the man will *fix the computers*. Sometimes, English speakers use the *when* adverbial clause by itself (e.g., *When I find time.*). However, such use creates an incomplete sentence because that adverbial clause *depends on* the second part of the sentence to create a complete sentence.

Expansion Activity: Practice *When* Clauses
(10 minutes)

Have students practice crafting *when* clauses by dividing the board into two sections, one labeled *situation* and the other labeled *action*. Elicit situations from students and their accompanying actions (e.g., *rain/umbrella; sun/sunscreen; school/books*). Then have students create sentences using those ideas. For example, they might write: *When it rains, I need an umbrella./I need an umbrella when it rains.; When the sun is out, I use sunscreen./I use sunscreen when the sun is out.*

A (10 minutes)

Direct students to write sentences to complete the activity. Call on volunteers to write a sentence on the board.

> **Activity A Answers, pp. 113–114**
> **1.** a. When I go out with my friends, I laugh a lot.
>   b. I laugh a lot when I go out with my friends.
> **2.** a. When you laugh, your blood pressure goes down.
>   b. Your blood pressure goes down when you laugh.
> **3.** a. When he sees something funny, he laughs.
>   b. He laughs when he sees something funny.
> **4.** a. When you laugh, you use calories.
>   b. You use calories when you laugh.
> **5.** a. When we hear a good joke, we laugh.
>   b. We laugh when we hear a good joke.
> **6.** a. When she is nervous, she laughs.
>   b. She laughs when she is nervous.

 Reading and Writing 1, page 114

B (10 minutes)

1. Read the directions aloud. Tell students to write sentences to complete the activity.

2. Have students share their sentences with a partner.

> **Activity B Answers, p. 114**
> Answers will vary. Possible answers:
> **1.** I laugh a lot when I am with friends.
> **2.** I never laugh when people are mean.
> **3.** When I see someone fall, I do not laugh.
> **4.** When I am in class, I always pay attention.
> **5.** When I am nerous, I am quiet.
> **6.** When I laugh, I feel happy.
> **7.** When I am with my family, I talk a lot.

web For additional practice with sentences with *when,* have students visit *Q Online Practice.*

Writing Skill:
Writing a topic sentence (5 minutes)

1. Tell students that they have learned how to identify a topic sentence in a paragraph and now it's time for them to learn to write one themselves. Ask for volunteers to read aloud one or two sentences of this presentation. Answer any questions.

2. Do the activity in the following Skill Note with your class.

3. Check comprehension by asking questions: *What does a topic sentence do? What is the topic sentence in the example? Why is a good topic sentence important to your writing?*

Skill Note

The topic sentence *tells us what the writer will tell us.* Without a topic sentence, it can sometimes be difficult for a reader to figure out what the writer's main point is. Therefore, to cut down on reader confusion, academic writers need to place topic sentences in the beginning of their paragraphs.

To help students practice this concept, write a list of four or five topics on the board (e.g., city history, school, the zoo, laughter). For each topic, students must write one sentence that would function as a topic sentence for a paragraph on that topic. For example, *The zoo is a great place for children to go during the summer* is a good topic sentence for the topic of *the zoo.* Practice with topic sentences will help students become more efficient and organized academic writers.

 Reading and Writing 1, page 115

A (10 minutes)

1. Direct students to match each topic sentence with the correct paragraph.

2. Put students in pairs to discuss their answers.

3. Call on volunteers to share their ideas with the class.

> **Activity A Answers, p. 115**
> **1.** a. When Bob is nervous, he laughs.
> **2.** d. Sam laughs to be friendly.
> **3.** b. Mark relaxes when he laughs.
> **4.** c. Paul laughs when he hears something funny.

B (5 minutes)

Read the directions aloud. Direct students to apply what they've learned and write a topic sentence for the paragraph. Ask for volunteers to share their topic sentences with the class.

> **Activity B Answers, p. 115**
> Lee really likes his laughing club.

web For additional practice with writing a topic sentence, have students visit *Q Online Practice.*

Unit Assignment: Write a paragraph about what makes someone laugh

Unit Question (5 minutes)

Refer students back to the ideas they discussed at the beginning of the unit about laughter. Ask: *What makes you or someone you know laugh?* Bring out the answers students wrote on poster paper at the beginning of the unit. Cue students if necessary by asking specific questions about the content of the unit: *Why is laughter important? What makes you laugh the hardest? What kinds of things do you find funny? What kinds of things are not funny?* Read the direction lines for the assignment together to ensure understanding.

Learning Outcome

1. Tie the Unit Assignment to the unit learning outcome. Say: *The outcome for this unit is to explain what makes you or someone you know laugh. This Unit Assignment is going to let you show your skill at writing paragraphs, using a topic sentence, and writing sentences with* when *and* because.

2. Explain that you are going to use a rubric similar to their Self-Assessment checklist on p. 118 to grade their Unit Assignment. You can also share a copy of the Unit Assignment Rubric (on p. 64 of this *Teacher's Handbook*) with the students.

Plan and Write

Brainstorm

A (10 minutes)

1. Read the directions aloud. Direct students to complete the chart.

Plan

B (10 minutes)

1. Direct students to complete the planning activity. Remind them that they may choose one of the topic sentences in B or create their own.

2. Have students complete the outline.

Critical Thinking Tip (1 minute)

1. Read the tip aloud.

2. Point out to students that outlining gives them an organized overview of the information that they are going to be present in their writing. It helps to ensure that no information is left out or misplaced.

Critical Q: Expansion Activity

Outlining

1. Explain to students: *A popular way to prepare to outline one's ideas is to use a cluster map. In a cluster map, a big circle is drawn in the middle of a page or on the board, and a main point is written inside it—**this will become the topic sentence in the outline.***

2. Then explain: *Next, lines are drawn away from the circle and new, smaller circles are attached to the other end of those lines. Inside each of the smaller circles, ideas are written which relate to the main point—**these become supporting sentences in the outline.***

3. Have students draw a cluster map to brainstorm ideas for their Unit Assignment. In the middle of the large circle can be *laughter,* and in the smaller circles can be words such as *jokes, friends,* etc.

4. Have students reference this cluster map to help them fill out the outline on p. 117 by expanding their ideas in the circles into complete topic and supporting sentences. Then have students restate their topic sentence in a concluding sentence.

Write

C (20 minutes)

After students finish the outline, direct them to read the directions silently and complete the activity.

Alternative Unit Assignments

Assign or have students choose one of these assignments to do instead of, or in addition to, the Unit Assignment.

1. Are you a funny person? What do you do to make people laugh? Write a paragraph explaining why you are or aren't funny.

2. Think of a friend who makes you laugh a lot. Write a paragraph about why you laugh a lot with this friend. Write about the situations that make you laugh and/or about things your friend does to make you laugh.

 For an additional unit assignment, have students visit *Q Online Practice*.

Revise and Edit

Peer Review

A (15–20 minutes)

1. Pair students and direct them to read each other's work.

2. Ask students to answer the questions and discuss them.

3. Give students suggestions of helpful feedback: *Your topic sentence should go before the supporting sentences. Try to use some of the vocabulary from this unit.*

Rewrite

B (15–20 minutes)

Students should review their partners' answers from A and rewrite their paragraphs if necessary.

▶ *Reading and Writing 1, page 118*

Edit

C (15–20 minutes)

1. Direct students to read and complete the Self-Assessment checklist. They should be prepared to hand in their work or discuss it in class.

2. Ask for a show of hands for how many students gave all or mostly *Yes* answers.

3. Use the Unit Assignment Rubric on p. 64 in this *Teacher's Handbook* to score each student's assignment.

4. Alternatively, divide the class into large groups and have students read their paragraphs to their group. (Make copies of each student's paragraph for each person in the group, to assist with scoring.) Pass out copies of the Unit Assignment Rubric and have students grade each other.

▶ *Reading and Writing 1, page 119*
Track Your Success (5 minutes)

1. Have students circle the words they have learned in this unit. Suggest that students go back through the unit to review any words they have forgotten.

2. Have students check the skills they have mastered. If students need more practice to feel confident about their proficiency in a skill, point out the pages numbers and encourage them to review.

3. Read the learning outcome aloud (*Explain what makes you or someone you know laugh*). Ask students if they feel that they have met the outcome.

Unit Assignment Rubric

Student name: _____

Date: _____

Unit Assignment: *Write a paragraph about what makes someone laugh.*

20 = Writing element was completely successful (at least 90% of the time).
15 = Writing element was mostly successful (at least 70% of the time).
10 = Writing element was partially successful (at least 50% of the time).
 0 = Writing element was not successful.

Writing a Paragraph	20 points	15 points	10 points	0 points
The first line of the paragraph is indented, and the paragraph has an appropriate topic sentence.				
Sentences with *when* and *because* are correct.				
Paragraph explains what makes someone laugh using vocabulary from the unit.				
Sentences begin with capital letters and end with appropriate punctuation.				
Every sentence has a subject and a verb and they are in agreement.				

Total points: _____

Comments:

Unit QUESTION

How does music make you feel?

Music

READING • identifying supporting sentences and details
VOCABULARY • the prefix *un-*
GRAMMAR • prepositions of location
WRITING • writing supporting sentences and details

LEARNING OUTCOME

Identify what type of music you like, where you listen to it, and how it makes you feel.

▶ *Reading and Writing 1, page 121*

Preview the Unit

Learning Outcome

1. Ask for a volunteer to read the unit skills, then the unit learning outcome.

2. Explain: *This is what you are expected to be able to do by the unit's end. The learning outcome explains how you are going to be evaluated. With this outcome in mind, you should focus on learning these skills (Reading, Vocabulary, Writing, Grammar) that will support your goal of identifying what type of music you like, where you listen to it, and how it makes you feel. This can also help you act as mentors in the classroom to help the other students meet this outcome.*

A (5 minutes)

1. Introduce the topic of music to the class. Tell them: *There are many kinds of music: pop, rock and roll, classical, and so on. Many people listen to music at home, when they're driving or riding the bus, or at concerts. Think about your day. When do you hear music?*

2. Put students in pairs or small groups to discuss the first two questions.

3. Call on volunteers to share their ideas with the class. Ask questions: *What kind of music does your partner like? What are some places that you know that play music?*

4. Focus students' attention on the photo. Read the third question aloud. Ask: *Where was this photo taken? What kind of dancing is this? Do you know people who dance in this style?*

Activity A Answers, p. 121
Answers will vary. Possible answers:
1. I listen to music at home when I do my homework. I hear music in the coffee shop.
2. My partner likes classical music. The pizza place always plays pop music.
3. This photo was taken outdoors, maybe near a subway or bus station. This is break dancing. I don't know anyone who dances this way.

B (5 minutes)

1. Introduce the Unit Question, *How does music make you feel?* Ask related information questions or questions about personal experience to help students prepare for answering the more abstract unit question. Ask: *What kind of music do you listen to when you feel happy? What about when you feel sad?*

2. Put students in small groups and give each group a piece of poster paper and a marker.

3. Read the Unit Question aloud. Give students a minute to silently consider their answers to the question. Tell students to pass the paper and marker around the group. Direct each group member to write an answer to the question. Encourage them to help one another.

4. Ask each group to choose a reporter to read the answers to the class. Point out similarities and differences among the answers. If answers from different groups are similar, make a group list that incorporates all of the answers. Post the list to refer to later in the unit.

Activity B Answers, p. 121
Answers will vary. Possible answers: Music makes me feel happy. Music always improves my mood. Music makes me forget about my problems.

The Q Classroom (5 minutes)

CD2, Track 05

1. Play The Q Classroom. Use the example from the audio to help students continue the conversation. Ask: *How did the students answer the question? Do you agree or disagree with their ideas? Why?*

2. In the Q classroom, Sophy says that she likes to listen to sad music when she is sad. Ask: *Do you like to listen to sad music when you are sad? Why or why not? How does music affect your moods?*

▶ *Reading and Writing 1, page 122*

C (10 minutes)

Ask for a volunteer to read the directions aloud. Put students in groups to complete the activity. You may want to do the first one together as an example.

D (10 minutes)

Direct students to complete the activity. Walk around the class as students discuss the questions in groups. Ask for volunteers to share their answers with the class.

EXPANSION ACTIVITY: Musical Moods (15 minutes)

1. Bring in several songs from different genres.

2. Play each song and ask students to describe how each song makes them feel by having them write one sentence for each song.

3. Model how a sentence can be written by writing a sentence on the board explaining how one of the songs make you feel.

4. After all songs have been played, pair students and have them share their sentences.

MULTILEVEL OPTION

Have higher-level students write two or three sentences describing their feelings as they hear each song.

READING

▶ *Reading and Writing 1, page 124*

READING 1: Music and Shopping

VOCABULARY (15 minutes)

1. Direct students to read the words and definitions. Model pronunciation and have students repeat the words.

2. Have students work with a partner to read the sentences and write the bolded words next to the correct definition.

3. Check answers as a class.

> **Vocabulary Answers, p. 125**
> a. customer; b. fit; c. exciting;
> d. volume; e. serious; f. notice;
> g. familiar; h. According to

 For additional practice with the vocabulary, have students visit *Q Online Practice*.

Tip for Success (1 minute)

1. Read the Tip for Success aloud.

2. Remind students that recognizing parts of speech is an important part of learning English.

PREVIEW READING 1 (5 minutes)

1. Read the directions aloud. Elicit or tell students what an *excerpt* is. Tell students to think for a moment before choosing an answer.

2. Tell students they should review their answer after reading.

> **Preview Reading 1 Answer, p. 124**
> the same amount

Reading 1 Background Note

Research conducted at the University of Bristol's Physiology Department in England suggests that no two people react to the same piece of music in the same way. However, there are observable patterns, and these patterns are used by marketers to influences customers habits. For example, most research subjects were amused when listening to banjo music. Many listeners felt annoyance at one piece of music: a violin being played by a beginner.

In the late 20th century, research was conducted at Southern Illinois University in the United States, which found that music did not have much of an effect on shoppers looking to purchase items that required a lot of thought—like a new house, new car, or insurance. Earlier research found that happier music created happier customers, but that sad music caused customers to increase their intention to buy items in the store. Clearly, the background music heard in stores is carefully chosen.

READ

🔊 CD2, Track 06

1. Instruct students to read the excerpt.

2. Play the audio and have students follow along.

▶ *Reading and Writing 1, page 125*

MAIN IDEAS (5 minutes)

1. When students are finished reading, direct them to read and complete the activity individually.

2. Ask for volunteers to share their answers.

> **Main Idea Answers, p. 125**
> **1.** c; **2.** c; **3.** a; **4.** b

▶ *Reading and Writing 1, page 126*

DETAILS (5 minutes)

1. Direct students to read the statements and complete the activity.

2. Have students compare answers with a partner.

3. Direct the students to look back at the article to check their answers.

4. Go over the answers with the class.

> **Details Answers, p. 126**
> **1.** b; **2.** a; **3.** a; **4.** a; **5.** b

Q WHAT DO YOU THINK? (20 minutes)

1. Ask students to read the questions and reflect on their answers.

2. Seat students in small groups and assign roles: a group leader to make sure everyone contributes, a note-taker to record the group's ideas, a reporter to share the group's ideas with the class, and a timekeeper to watch the clock.

3. Give students five minutes to discuss the questions. Call time if conversations are winding down. Allow them an extra minute or two if necessary.

4. Call on each group's reporter to share ideas with the class.

5. Have each student choose one of the questions and write two or three sentences in response.

6. Call on volunteers to share their ideas with the class.

> **What Do You Think? Answers, p. 126**
> Answers will vary.

 For additional practice with reading comprehension, have students visit *Q Online Practice*.

▶ *Reading and Writing 1, page 127*

Reading Skill: Identifying supporting sentences and details (10 minutes)

1. Present the reading skill. Elicit differences between *supporting sentences* and *details*. Include the content of the following Skill Note if you feel it will help.

2. Model meanings of *supporting sentences* and *details* using texts that you have with you: this book, the textbook, other books, newspapers, magazines, etc.

3. Check comprehension by asking questions: *What do good readers look for? What do supporting sentences support? What do details support? How do details support supporting sentences?*

Skill Note

The human body can be seen as a metaphor for paragraphs: you need bones and muscle to make the whole thing stay together. In a paragraph, the topic and supporting sentences are the bones. Without these sentences, there is no structure to the paragraph. However, without details, there is no form to the structure—there is no "muscle." The details are what give strength and depth to the paragraph, much like muscles give strength and depth to the human body. A body needs both bones and muscles, and so do paragraphs.

Practice this academic writing skill by pairing students and giving them a paragraph that has a topic sentence, supporting sentences, and details. Have students find and label these various sentences in the paragraph. Check answers as a class.

A (5 minutes)

1. Direct students to read and follow the directions to complete the activity. Students will compare their work with a partner.

2. When everyone is finished, check to see if there are any questions.

> **Reading Skill A Answers, p. 127**
> **Topic sentence for paragraph 4:** The kind of music a store plays can change a customer's sense of time. **Two supporting sentences for paragraph 4:** According to studies, familiar music gives shoppers a good idea of time. When customers hear music that is *not* familiar, they don't notice the time.; **Topic sentence for paragraph 5:** The kind of music a store plays can have an effect on the shopper's thoughts and feelings. **Two supporting sentences for paragraph 5:** Many stores play old, happy music so customers feel good. When customers hear *new* music, they forget about the world outside of the store.

Tip for Success (1 minute)

1. Read the Tip for Success.
2. Tell students that labeling parts of the paragraph is a great way to continually think about how paragraphs are formed. Encourage students to label often—maybe every time they read.

▶ *Reading and Writing 1, page 128*

B (5 minutes)

1. Read the directions aloud. Ask students to confirm their understanding of the activity by telling you what they need to do.
2. When students finish, check answers as a class.

> **Reading Skill B Answers, p. 128**
> **Paragraph 2:** 1. TS; 2. SS; 3. D; 4. D; 5. SS; 6. D; 7. SS
> **Paragraph 3:** 8. TS; 9. SS; 10. SS; 11. D; 12. D

 For additional practice with identifying supporting sentences and details, have students visit *Q Online Practice*.

Critical Thinking Tip (3 minutes)

1. Read the Critical Thinking Tip aloud.
2. Explain: *Learning to differentiate can help you understand ideas better, improving your vocabulary and general comprehension.*

Critical Q: Expansion Activity

Differentiating

1. Bring in various pictures of people's faces that showcase different emotions.
2. Show one picture at a time and have students write a word that summarizes the person's emotions (e.g., sad, happy, scared). Depending on proficiency levels in class, you may want to write a list of adjectives on the board that matches the emotions in the pictures.
3. After showing the pictures, show each one again, one by one, and have students reveal the emotion they paired with each picture. Discuss the concept of differentiation based upon the students' answers.

Learning Outcome

Use the learning outcome to frame the purpose and relevance of Reading 1. Ask: *What did you learn from Reading 1 that prepares you to identify what type of music you like, where you listen to it, and how it makes you feel? What did you learn that will help you with this identification?*

▶ *Reading and Writing 1, page 129*

READING 2: Music and the Movies

VOCABULARY (10 minutes)

1. Write vocabulary words on the board in two or three sections. Each section features all bolded vocabulary words. Divide the class into as many groups as there are sections on the board and line groups up an equal distance from the board. When you read a definition, a member of each team at the front of the line should run up to the board and "slap" the word to which the definition refers.
2. Correct as necessary. The "runner" rewrites any words that have been erased and goes to the back of his or her group's line. Repeat until students "slap" correct words most of the time.

> **Vocabulary Answers, p. 129**
> **1.** perfectly;   **2.** character;   **3.** instrument;
> **4.** scene;   **5.** action;   **6.** level;
> **7.** tense;   **8.** composer;   **9.** director

 For additional practice with the vocabulary, have students visit *Q Online Practice*.

> **MULTILEVEL OPTION**
>
> Have lower-level students rewrite the words that are "slapped" off the board.
> Have higher-level students provide an example sentence with the vocabulary item they "slap."

▶ *Reading and Writing 1, page 130*

PREVIEW READING 2 (5 minutes)

1. Direct students to read the question and check one answer.
2. Tell students they should review their answer after reading.

> **Preview Reading 2, p. 130**
> Answers will vary.

Reading 2 Background Note

Howard Shore, born in Canada in 1946, is an Oscar-winning composer. He has created film scores for many films including: *Doubt* (2008), *The Departed* (2006), and *The Lord of the Rings: The Fellowship of the Ring* (2001).

John Williams, born in the United States in 1932, is also an Oscar-winning composer. He has created film scores for many films including *Star Wars* (1977). Williams has also composed themes for four Olympic games—1984, 1988, 1996, and 2002.

Michiru Ōshima, born in the Japan in 1961, is a film, TV, and video game score composer. She has created music for films such as: *Memories of Tomorrow* (2007) and *Like Asura* (2004); TV shows such as the animated *Fullmetal Alchemist*; and video games such as *The Legend of Zelda: Twilight Princess*.

READ

🔊 CD2, Track 07

1. Instruct students to read the article.
2. Play the audio and have students follow along.

▶ *Reading and Writing 1, page 131*

MAIN IDEAS (5 minutes)

1. Read the directions aloud.
2. Ask students to read and complete the activity individually.
3. Go over the answers as a class, asking for volunteers to explain their reasoning.

> **Main Idea Answers, p. 131**
> **Paragraph 2:** a. TS; b. SS;
> **Paragraph 3:** a. SS; b. TS;
> **Paragraph 4:** a. SS; b. TS;
> **Paragraph 5:** a. TS; b. SS

▶ *Reading and Writing 1, page 132*

DETAILS

A (5 minutes)

1. Direct students to read the statements and complete the activity.
2. Have students compare answers with a partner.
3. Direct the students to look back at the article to check their answers.
4. Go over the answers with the class.

> **Details A Answers, p. 132**
> **1.** T; **2.** F; **3.** T; **4.** T; **5.** T; **6.** F

B (10 minutes)

Direct students to order the steps to complete the activity. Ask students to check their answers with a partner before going over the answers as a class.

> **Details B Answers, p. 132**
> **a.** 2; **b.** 4; **c.** 1; **d.** 3

 For additional practice with reading comprehension, have students visit *Q Online Practice*.

Q WHAT DO YOU THINK?

A (10 minutes)

1. Ask students to read the questions and reflect on their answers.
2. Seat students in small groups and assign roles: a group leader to make sure everyone contributes, a note-taker to record the group's ideas, a reporter to share the group's ideas with the class, and, if there are enough students, a timekeeper to watch the clock.
3. Give students five minutes to discuss the questions. Call time if conversations are winding down. Allow them an extra minute or two if necessary.

> **Activity A Answers, p. 132**
> **1.** Answers will vary.
> **2.** Answers will vary. Possible answers: I like the music in *Gladiator* because it is beautiful. I like the music in *Transformers* because it is loud and fast.

B (10 minutes)

1. Tell the students that they should think about both Reading 1 and Reading 2 as they answer the questions in B.
2. Ask students to discuss the questions with their group.
3. Call on each group to share ideas with the class.

> **Activity B Answers, p. 132**
> Answers will vary. Possible answers:
> **1.** Yes, because I have to like the music to like the movie.
> **2.** Action movies, because the music keeps you interested.

Learning Outcome

Use the learning outcome to frame the purpose and relevance of Readings 1 and 2 and the Critical Q activity. Ask: *What did you learn from Reading 2 that prepares you to identify what type of music you like, where you listen to it, and how it makes you feel?*

▶ *Reading and Writing 1, page 133*

Vocabulary Skill: The prefix *un-* (5 minutes)

1. Present information to students. Present students with several different prefixes and their related words (e.g., *dis-* and *disappear*) from the Skill Note below. Ask: *Which of these prefixes have you seen before? How do you think these prefixes change the meaning of the words?* Point out that prefixes can be added to adjectives, nouns, and verbs.

2. Check comprehension: *What is a prefix? How does the meaning change when you add* un- *to an adjective? What are some other words you know that have the prefix* un-? Re-?

3. Have students put prefixes *un-* and *re-* in front of words they already know to see if they can discover new words. Have students write their ideas on the board and correct as needed.

Skill Note

Prefixes are a strong, quick way to increase a student's vocabulary two- or three-fold. Simply by adding a few letters to the beginning of an already-known adjective, students can begin experimenting and using new vocabulary items quite quickly. Here are a few more prefixes that students can practice adding to adjectives:

Prefix	Meaning	Example
dis-	not	*dis*appear
pre-	before	*pre*view
re-	again	*re*write

Here are a few prefixes that you can add to nouns:

Prefix	Meaning	Example
non-	absence	*non*-smoker
pro-	in support of	*pro*-school
anti-	against	*anti*-drug

Have students practice using these prefixes with adjectives and nouns that they already know. This will help them realize that they can increase their vocabulary with short, simple prefixes.

A (10 minutes)

1. Read the directions aloud. Discuss the two examples. Direct students to complete the activity with a dictionary.

2. Go over the answers with the class.

> **Activity A Answers, p. 133**
> **1.** not bored;   **2.** unfriendly;   **3.** unhappy;
> **4.** unimportant;   **5.** unintelligent;   **6.** unnatural;
> **7.** not quiet;   **8.** unpopular;   **9.** not similar;
> **10.** unusual

MULTILEVEL OPTION

Have higher-level students work with lower-level students to write sentences—one for each adjective in Activity A. Have students write some of their sentences on the board. As time permits, correct the sentences individually, then in pairs, then as a class, practicing class editing skills.

B (10 minutes)

1. Ask for a volunteer to read the directions aloud.

2. Do the first sentence together as an example. Ask students to check their answers with a partner before going over the answers as a class.

> **Activity B Answers, p. 133**
> Answers will vary.

 For additional practice with the prefix *un-*, have students visit *Q Online Practice*.

▶ *Reading and Writing 1, page 134*

WRITING

Grammar: Prepositions of location
(5 minutes)

1. Read the description of the grammar skill aloud, focusing on one bullet at a time. Ask for volunteers to read the prepositional phrases.

2. As you present the bullets, elicit examples from students of times when they use the words *in*, *on*, and *at*. Write a few of their examples on the board.

3. Write a few example sentences on the board: *I'm at school. My friend is in a band. I fell asleep on the bus yesterday.* Have students select the preposition of location from these sentences. Create more examples as needed or if time permits.

4. Do the activity in the following Skill Note.

5. Check comprehension: *What does a preposition of location do? When can we use* at*? Which preposition should you use with large areas like countries?*

Skill Note

Prepositions of location are some of the most common words in English. *In* ranks as the 6th most common word in English, *on* ranks as the 14th most common, and *at* ranks 22nd. Because these words are so common, students will come across them often, giving them many opportunities to become familiar with them. However, these prepositions are also used in *phrasal verbs* (e.g., *get at, go on,* and *jump in*) so their appearance in texts can sometimes be confusing for students.

Help students recognize *on, in,* and *at* by giving them texts where they appear as prepositions of location and asking them to highlight them. The more that students recognize the placement of the prepositions in texts, the more comfortable students will be reading and using these prepositions—and others—in context.

A (5 minutes)

1. Direct students to read the directions and complete the sentences. Have students check their answers with a partner.

> **Activity A Answers, p. 134**
> **1.** at; **2.** on; **3.** at; **4.** on; **5.** in; **6.** in;
> **7.** at; **8.** at

▶ *Reading and Writing 1, page 135*

B (10 minutes)

1. Read the directions aloud.

2. Have students write their answers.

3. Direct students to discuss their answers with a partner. Ask for volunteers to share their answers with the class.

Activity B Answers, p. 135
Answers will vary. Possible answers:
1. I like to listen to music on the subway.
2. I like to listen to music with my friends.
3. I like to listen to music in my car.
4. I don't like to listen to music at the library.
5. I don't like to listen to music at night.

 For additional practice with prepositions of location, have students visit *Q Online Practice.*

Writing Skill: Writing supporting sentences and details (5 minutes)

1. Tell students that they've learned how to identify supporting sentences and details in a paragraph and now it's time for them to learn to write them themselves.

2. Have students read information in pairs. Each pair should focus on one of the topics: *supporting sentences* or *details.* Then put pairs together so that they teach each other about their topic. (Those who read *supporting details* teach that information to the pair that read *details* and vice versa.)

3. Do the activity in the following Skill Note.

4. Check comprehension by asking questions: *What do supporting sentences do? Reasons, facts, and dates are kinds of what? What's the difference between the supporting sentences and details in the sample paragraph? What are some other details that could be added to this paragraph?*

Skill Note

Paragraphs are like arguments: You need facts to support your ideas which then support the main part of the argument. For example, your boss wants you to stay late at work, but you can't because you have to pick up your daughter from school (the topic sentence of your argument). You are the only one available to pick up your daughter (supporting sentence) because you have the only car (detail). Furthermore, your daughter needs you to meet with her teacher after school today (supporting sentence) because you have to sign a form for her to be able to participate in an after-school activity tomorrow (detail). Thus, you cannot stay late at work because your daughter is depending on you (restating the topic sentence).

Students can transfer skills they already possess in their social lives into their academic writing lives. In life, people often make well-reasoned, detailed *oral* arguments for or against certain ideas. Some people might even make such arguments every day, and find that they are good at getting their points across. Such skills can translate into paragraph writing.

A (10 minutes)

1. Direct students to read the directions and complete the activity.

2. Put students in pairs to discuss their answers.

3. Call on volunteers to share their ideas with the class.

> **Activity A Answers, p. 135**
> Supporting sentences:
>   I like to listen to classical music at work.
>   I like to listen to fast and loud music in the car.
>   I like to listen to string music in bed.
> Details:
>   It makes me feel intelligent and serious.
>   It makes me feel energetic and happy.
>   It makes me feel quiet and relaxed.

▶ *Reading and Writing 1, page 136*

B (5 minutes)

Read the directions aloud. Direct students to complete the activity by writing the appropriate supporting sentences on the lines. Check their understanding by doing the first line of item 1 together.

> **Activity B Answers, p. 136**
> **1.** a, d;   **2.** b, c

C (5 minutes)

Ask for a volunteer to read the directions aloud. Direct students to complete the activity by writing the appropriate details on the lines.

> **Activity C Answers, p. 136**
> **1.** c, b;   **2.** a, d

 For additional practice with writing supporting sentences and details, have students visit *Q Online Practice*

Q Unit Assignment: Write a paragraph about how music makes you feel

▶ *Reading and Writing 1, page 137*

Unit Question (5 minutes)

Refer students back to the ideas they discussed at the beginning of the unit about music. Cue students if necessary by asking specific questions about the content of the unit: *What kind of music do you like to listen to? Where are some places around town that you hear music? Do you listen to different kinds of music depending on your mood?* Read the direction lines for the assignment together to ensure understanding.

Learning Outcome

1. Tie the Unit Assignment to the unit learning outcome. Say: *The outcome for this unit is to identify what kind of music you like, where you listen to it, and how it makes you feel. This Unit Assignment is going to let you show your skill at writing paragraphs, using supporting sentences, details, and prepositions of location.*

2. Explain that you are going to use a rubric similar to their Self-Assessment checklist on p. 138 to grade their Unit Assignment. You can also share a copy of the Unit Assignment Rubric (on p. 75 of this *Teacher's Handbook*) with the students.

Plan and Write

Brainstorm

A (10 minutes)

Read the directions aloud. Refer students to the checklist on p. 138 to guide their brainstorming. Direct students to write their ideas on the lines and then share them with a partner.

Tip for Success (1 minute)

Read the Tip for Success. Ensure that students place their topic sentences as the first or second sentence in their paragraphs. A hook, which is a sentence that grabs the reader's attention, can precede the topic sentence.

Plan

B (10 minutes)

Direct students to complete the planning activity. Remind them to use vocabulary words from the unit.

Your Writing Process (1 minute)

1. Read the Your Writing Process tip aloud.
2. Encourage students to use *Q Online Practice* frequently.

Write

C (10 minutes)

Direct students to write their paragraph in their notebook, referring to the checklist on p. 138.

Alternative Unit Assignments

Assign or have students choose one of these assignments to do instead of, or in addition to, the Unit Assignment.

1. Keep a music diary. Write down all the places you hear music in one day. Write down how you feel in each place. For example:

Place	Kind of Music	I feel...
1. supermarket	popular music	happy

Then write a paragraph about the music in one or more of the places and how it made you feel.

2. Watch a scene of a movie that has music. Describe how the scene feels with sound. Then watch the same scene with no sound. Now write a paragraph about how the scene feels with no sound.

 For an additional unit assignment, have students visit *Q Online Practice*.

▶ *Reading and Writing 1, page 138*

Revise and Edit

Peer Review

A (15–20 minutes)

1. Pair students and direct them to read each other's work.
2. Ask students to answer the questions and discuss them.
3. Give students suggestions of helpful feedback: *Your topic sentence is too specific; try to make it more general. I liked your first supporting sentence and detail. Your details should come after the supporting sentence.*

Rewrite

B (15–20 minutes)

Students should review their partners' answers from A and rewrite their paragraphs if necessary.

C (15–20 minutes)

1. Direct students to read and complete the Self-Assessment checklist. They should be prepared to hand in their work or discuss it in class.

2. Ask for a show of hands for how many students gave all or mostly *Yes* answers.

3. Use the Unit Assignment Rubric on p. 75 in this *Teacher's Handbook* to score each student's assignment.

4. Alternatively, divide the class into large groups and have students read their paragraphs to their group. (Make copies of each student's writing for each person in the group, to assist with scoring.) Pass out copies of the Unit Assignment Rubric and have students grade each other.

▶ *Reading and Writing 1, page 139*

Track Your Success (5 minutes)

1. Have students circle the words they have learned in this unit. Suggest that students go back through the unit to review any words they have forgotten.

2. Have students check the skills they have mastered. If students need more practice to feel confident about their proficiency in a skill, point out the pages numbers and encourage them to review.

3. Read the learning outcome aloud (*Identify what type of music you like, where you listen to it, and how it makes you feel*). Ask students if they feel that they have met the outcome.

Unit Assignment Rubric

Student name: _____

Date: _____

Unit Assignment: *Write a paragraph about how music makes you feel.*

20 = Writing element was completely successful (at least 90% of the time).
15 = Writing element was mostly successful (at least 70% of the time).
10 = Writing element was partially successful (at least 50% of the time).
 0 = Writing element was not successful.

Writing a Paragraph	20 points	15 points	10 points	0 points
The first line of the paragraph is indented; sentences begin with capital letters and end with appropriate punctuation.				
Prepositions of location are correct.				
Supporting sentences and details clearly identify how music makes the student feel.				
The paragraph includes vocabulary from the unit.				
Spelling is correct.				

Total points: _____

Comments:

8

Unit QUESTION
Is it ever OK to lie?

Honesty

READING • identifying pronoun referents
VOCABULARY • collocations
WRITING • writing concluding sentences
GRAMMAR • infinitives of purpose

LEARNING OUTCOME

Write a paragraph that explains your opinion about whether or not it is OK to lie in an online forum.

▶ *Reading and Writing 1, page 141*

Preview the Unit

Learning Outcome

1. Ask for a volunteer to read the unit skills, then the unit learning outcome. Make sure students understand what an *online forum* is.

2. Explain: *This is what you are expected to be able to do by the unit's end. The learning outcome explains how you are going to be evaluated. With this outcome in mind, you should focus on learning these skills (Reading, Vocabulary, Writing, Grammar) that will support your goal of writing a paragraph that explains your opinion about whether or not it is OK to lie in an online forum. This can also help you act as mentors in the classroom to help the other students meet this outcome.*

A (5 minutes)

1. Introduce the topic of honesty to the class. Check that students understand the meaning of *honesty, to tell the truth,* and *a lie.* Ask: *What do you think about people who lie?*

2. Put students in pairs or small groups to discuss the first two questions in A.

3. Call on volunteers to share their ideas with the class. Ask questions: *Why do you think children lie more than adults? If you think that adults lie more than children, why do you think that is? Is there a difference between the lies of children and of adults? What kind of difference?*

4. Focus students' attention on the photo. Have a volunteer describe the photo to the class. Read the third question aloud. Ask: *What kind of mood is this woman in? How do you know? What is in her hand?*

Activity A Answers, p. 141
Answers will vary. Possible answers:
1. Adults lie more than children. Children lie more than adults. Children and adults lie the same amount.
2. I think children lie because they don't want to get in trouble. Adults lie because they want to make other people feel good. Children lie about simple things but adults lie about more complex things.
3. This woman looks like she is in a meeting. Maybe the person she's talking to is telling a lie. She is holding a piece of paper.

B (15 minutes)

1. Introduce the Unit Question, *Is it ever OK to lie?* Ask related information questions or questions about personal experience to help students prepare for answering the more abstract Unit Question. Ask: *If a relative gives you a present that you don't like, should you lie and say you like it? If the truth will make someone feel bad, is it OK to lie?*

2. Read the Unit Question aloud. Give students a minute to silently consider their answers to the question. Then ask students who would answer *yes* to stand on one side of the room and students who would answer *no* to stand on the other side of the room.

3. Direct students to tell a partner next to them their reasons for choosing that side of the issue.

4. Call on volunteers from each side to share their opinions with the class.

5. After students have shared their opinions, provide an opportunity for anyone who would like to change sides to do so.

6. Ask students to sit down, copy the Unit Question, and make a note of students' answers and their reasons. They will refer back to these notes at the end of the unit.

Answers will vary. Possible answers: If a relative gives me a present I don't like, I would probably lie so that he/she doesn't feel bad. I think there are some times when it is OK to lie.

The Q Classroom (5 minutes)

CD2, Track 08

1. Play The Q Classroom. Use the example from the audio to help students continue the conversation. Ask: *How did the students answer the question? Do you agree or disagree with their ideas? Why?*

2. In the audio, Sophy says that lies that don't hurt anybody are fine. Ask: *What are examples of lies that don't hurt someone? How do you know if a lie doesn't hurt? What lies have you been told that don't hurt?*

▶ *Reading and Writing 1, page 142*

C (20 minutes)

1. Ask for a volunteer to read the directions aloud. Put students in pairs to complete the activity.

2. Call on students to share their answers with the class. Ask: *Why did you choose the answer that you did?*

3. Give students time to role play the situations.

D (10 minutes)

Direct students to read the directions and complete the activity. When they finish the survey, put them in small groups to compare and discuss answers.

EXPANSION ACTIVITY: Two Truths and a Lie (10 minutes)

1. Have students write down two truths and one lie about themselves on a slip of paper.

2. Group students and have one student at a time read their list to their group. After the student reads his or her statements, the rest of the group has to guess which statement is a lie. Have students keep reading until all students in all groups have read their statements aloud.

3. Choose two or three volunteers to read their statements to the class, having students who were not in that person's group guess which statement is a lie.

READING

▶ *Reading and Writing 1, page 143*

READING 1: The Lies People Tell

VOCABULARY (10 minutes)

1. Read the directions aloud.

2. Have students read the bold vocabulary words and their definitions. Direct students to complete the sentences with the bold words.

3. Check answers as a class.

Vocabulary Answers, p. 143
1. trouble;   2. furniture;   3. punishment;
4. fire;   5. control;   6. admit;
7. reputation;   8. boss;   9. continue

 For additional practice with the vocabulary, have students visit *Q Online Practice*.

MULTILEVEL OPTION

Group lower-level students and assist them with the task. Provide alternate example sentences to help them understand the words. Use these example sentences for more difficult vocabulary. *There must be some kind of* **punishment** *for hitting his sister. The* **punishment** *for murder in some countries is death. I don't want to* **fire** *you, but your actions are inappropriate. Many people do not like to* **admit** *that they made a mistake.*

Have higher-level students complete the activity individually and then compare answers with a partner. Tell the pairs to write an additional sample sentence for each expression. Have volunteers write one of their sentences on the board. Correct the sentences with the whole class, focusing on the use of the expression rather than other grammatical issues.

▶ *Reading and Writing 1, page 144*

PREVIEW READING 1 (5 minutes)

1. Read the directions aloud to the class. Tell them to think for a moment before choosing their answers.

2. Tell students they should review their answer after reading.

Preview Reading 1 Answer, p. 144
the lies people often tell; why people tell lies

Reading 1 Background Note

Psychologist Robert Feldman, who works at the University of Massachusetts in the United States, notes that lying is tied to self-esteem (i.e., self-worth or self-respect). When self-esteem is threatened (one's own or someone else's), people tend to lie to protect it. These type of lies are not typically unkind. For example, few people would say that a woman who sleeps through her alarm but tells everyone she is a light sleeper is being hurtful with her lie. Instead, she is creating an image of herself that she wants to be or wants people to believe about her. Interestingly, according to research done at the University of Alberta in Canada, people tend to lie to people that they know but not to strangers. This finding makes sense if we see lying as connected to self-esteem. Few people care what a stranger thinks of them; however, most people care what co-workers or friends think about them.

READD

READ

🔊 CD2, Track 09

1. Instruct students to read the article.

2. Play the audio and have students follow along.

▶ *Reading and Writing 1, page 145*

MAIN IDEAS (5 minutes)

1. When students are finished reading, direct students to read and complete the activity individually.

2. Ask for volunteers to share their answers.

> **Main Idea Answers, p. 145**
> 2; 3; 5; 6; 7; 8; 10

▶ *Reading and Writing 1, page 146*

DETAILS (5 minutes)

1. Direct students to read the statements and complete the activity.

2. Have students compare answers with a partner.

3. Direct the students to look back at the article to check their answers.

4. Go over the answers with the class.

> **Details Answers, p. 146**
> **1.** a;   2. a;   3. b;   4. a

 For additional practice with reading comprehension, have students visit *Q Online Practice.*

Q WHAT DO YOU THINK? (15 minutes)

1. Ask students to read the lies and reflect on their answers. For A, they should fill out the chart individually with their opinions, referring back to the reading as needed.

2. For B, seat students in small groups and assign roles: a group leader to make sure everyone contributes, a note-taker to record the group's ideas, a reporter to share the group's ideas with the class, and a timekeeper to watch the clock.

3. Give students five minutes to discuss the questions. Call time if conversations are winding down. Allow them an extra minute or two if necessary.

4. Call on each group's reporter to share ideas with the class.

5. Have each student choose one of the questions and write 3–4 sentences in response.

6. Call on volunteers to share ideas with the class.

> **What Do You Think? Answers, p. 146**
> Answers will vary.

EXPANSION ACTIVITY: Interview (10–15 minutes)

1. For homework, have students interview two or three people outside of class, asking them, *Which kinds of lies are OK to tell?* Have students write down the answers they hear. (Or have students translate the answers they receive if the interviewee doesn't speak English.)

2. The next day, have students share their answers in pairs and then with the class. Ask: *Did you get any surprising answers? Do you agree with any of the answers? Why? Do you disagree with any of the answers? Why?*

Learning Outcome

Use the learning outcome to frame the purpose and relevance of Reading 1. Ask: *What did you learn from Reading 1 that prepares you to write a paragraph that explains your opinion about whether or not it is OK to lie in an online forum?*

Reading Skill:
Identifying pronoun referents (15 minutes)

1. Present (or review) subject and object pronouns. Quiz students by asking: *Who can tell me all of the subject pronouns? Who can tell me all of the object pronouns?*

2. Provide practice with referents. Write the following two sentences on the board: *My brother Matt is a great person. He likes to help everyone with their homework.* Ask the class: *Which noun does he refer to?* (Answer: Matt). Try a few more examples to give students the idea of referents. *The neighbor is very noisy. She often plays loud music at night.; Our dog is playful. He never gets tired of chasing after balls.*

3. Do the activity in the Skill Note below with the class.

4. Check comprehension by asking questions: *What is a pronoun? What is the difference between the two kinds of pronouns? What is a pronoun referent and why is it useful?*

Skill Note

Pronouns act as shortcuts for writers (and speakers) to refer back to a noun in the sentence (or the previous sentence). Typically, pronouns are not placed very far away from the noun they are referring to. However, a common error is to place the pronoun referent directly after the noun it refers to (e.g., *Nancy she is working.; Sayid he knows the answer.*). Remind students that pronouns *stand in for* nouns, but they should not stand <u>directly</u> next to the nouns they refer to.

To practice, choose a reading in the student book and ask students to underline all of the pronouns that they see. Then ask students if they can find the noun that those pronoun referents refer to. Lead the class in a discussion of how they know that those nouns and their pronoun referents are connected.

A (5 minutes)

1. Direct students to read and follow the directions to complete the activity.

2. Students may compare their work with a partner and discuss any differences they find. When everyone is finished, check to see if there are any questions.

Reading Skill A Answers, p. 148
1. People; 2. A small lie; 3. Children;
4. Janet Cooke; 5. his stories

B (5 minutes)

1. Read the directions aloud. Ask students to confirm their understanding of the activity by telling you what they need to do.

2. When students finish, check answers as a class.

Reading Skill B Answers, p. 148
1. a. hair, b. husband, c. woman;
2. a. Pete, b. boss, c. Lina;
3. a. cat, b. parents, c. truth;
4. a. boy, b. sister, c. parents

 For additional practice with identifying pronoun referents, have students visit *Q Online Practice.*

READING 2: Honesty and Parenting

VOCABULARY (10 minutes)

1. Write bolded vocabulary on the board and probe for prior knowledge. *What words do you already know? What do those words mean?*

2. Put students in groups of two or three and have them complete the activity. Encourage students to make guesses and emphasize that it's OK to be wrong. Circulate around the class and answer questions as needed.

3. When groups have finished working, provide or elicit correct answers.

Vocabulary Answers, p. 149
a. opinion;   **b.** respect;
c. require;   **d.** avoid;
e. trust;   **f.** practice;
g. purpose;   **h.** relationship

 For additional practice with the vocabulary, have students visit *Q Online Practice.*

MULTILEVEL OPTION
Place students in mixed-ability pairs. The higher-level students can assist lower-level students with the activity and explain their understanding of the meaning of the words. Direct students to alternate reading the sentences aloud. Encourage them to help each other with pronunciation.

PREVIEW READING 2 (5 minutes)

1. Read the directions aloud. Ask for a volunteer to remind the class what it means to skim the reading. Direct students to read the question and check one answer.

2. Tell students they should review their answer after reading.

> **Preview Reading 2 Answer, p. 150**
> not telling the truth to her son

Tip for Success (1 minute)

Read the tip aloud. Remind students that mistakes are important. As we make mistakes in writing and speaking, we learn how language works. Each mistake gives us information to improve our skills, and mistakes now translate into success in the future. Not all chat rooms are appropriate for students, so make sure to monitor your students if you choose to have them work in chat rooms in the classroom.

Reading 2 Background Note

"White lies" are built into many societies. They are not meant to hurt anyone, but some people argue that white lies erode trust—especially between parents and their children. Some parents tell white lies because they know the truth can be difficult, especially for young children. Parents want to protect their children.

READ

🔊 CD2, Track 10

1. Instruct students to read the posts.

2. Play the audio and have students follow along.

MAIN IDEAS (5 minutes)

1. Read the directions aloud.

2. Ask students to read and complete the activity individually.

3. Go over the answers as a class, asking for volunteers to support their answers with examples from the reading.

> **Main Idea Answers, p. 151**
> **1.** Yes; **2.** No; **3.** No; **4.** No; **5.** Yes;
> **6.** No; **7.** No

DETAILS (5 minutes)

1. Direct students to read the directions and fill in the chart to complete the activity.

2. Have students compare answers with a partner.

3. Direct the students to look back at the chat room posts to check their answers.

4. Go over the answers with the class.

> **Details Answers, p. 152**
> Answers will vary. Possible answers: Reasons It's OK to Lie: Your purpose was to make him feel good, white lies are a necessary part of life, we need to lie to avoid hurting each other.; Reasons It's not OK to Lie: Honesty is the first step to a good parent-child relationship, the truth will make him strong, every lie requires more lies, children learn honesty from example.

 For additional practice with reading comprehension, have students visit *Q Online Practice*.

21ST CENTURY SKILLS

Being open to other people, ideas, opinions, and beliefs—and incorporating them into a successful group atmosphere—is an important skill to have and develop in the 21st century. Not everyone is going to agree all the time on a given topic. Sometimes, in disagreement, new solutions arise that might not have arisen if everyone shared the same opinion. It is important to engage with people who disagree so that a solution that the entire group agrees upon can be found.

This unit's discussion of whether or not it is OK to lie, and of people's differing comfort levels with lying, provides an opportunity to practice being open to conflicting or differing perspectives. Have students pair with other students who do not share their same opinions about the value of lying. Ask them to respond to their partners' opposing positions by practicing *active listening skills*. Encourage students to use phrases like *I understand what you're saying* or *What I'm hearing you say is…*[insert summary of partner's opinion]. Emphasize that they need to make their partners feel like they are being listened to and understood. Encourage the listeners not to interrupt with their own opinions.

WHAT DO YOU THINK?

A (10 minutes)

1. Ask students to read the questions and reflect on their answers.

2. Seat students in small groups and assign roles: a group leader to make sure everyone contributes, a note-taker to record the group's ideas, a reporter to share the group's ideas with the class, and a timekeeper to watch the clock.

3. Give students five minutes to discuss the questions. Call time if conversations are winding down. Allow them an extra minute or two if necessary.

> **Activity A Answers, p. 152**
> Answers will vary. Possible answers:
> **1.** I agree with Missy that Marisa missed the chance to teach her son an important lesson.
> **2.** I disagree with HueyBoy that Marisa worries too much and that sometimes lying is necessary.

B (10 minutes)

1. Tell the students that they should think about both Reading 1 and Reading 2 as they answer the questions in B.

2. Ask students to discuss their answers in a group.

3. Call on each group's reporter to share ideas with the class.

> **Activity B Answers, p. 152**
> Answers will vary. Possible answers:
> **1.** Parents sometimes lie about what happened to their pets or if they're good at sports.
> **2.** I think white lies are OK because they don't hurt anyone and they make children feel better.

Learning Outcome

Use the learning outcome to frame the purpose and relevance of Reading 2. Ask: *What did you learn from Reading 2 that prepares you to write a paragraph that explains your opinion about whether or not it is OK to lie in an online forum?*

Vocabulary Skill: Collocations (10 minutes)

1. Present information on collocations to students. Explain that there are patterns to how words are used in sentences. Elicit/provide examples of collocation patterns students (or you) know. (e.g., *Brush your teeth* instead of *comb your teeth)*. Search "BYU English Corpus" on an Internet search engine to find an online English corpus that students can use to find more patterns. Follow the activity in the following Skill Note for more practice.

2. Check comprehension: *What are collocations? Where can you find information about collocation patterns* (e.g., dictionaries, online corpora)? *How will learning collocations help you? Can you think of some other collocations like* make the bed *and* do the dishes?

Tip for Success (1 minute)

1. Read the tip aloud.

2. Tell students that they can search for collocation information on the Internet. Doing an online search for an English corpus will bring students to an online engine for finding collocation patterns with any word in English.

Skill Note

Students often express a desire to "speak like a native speaker," and understanding collocation patterns is a sure way of moving toward that goal. When students learn a new word, like *purpose* from this unit, referencing the words that *purpose* typically collocates with gives students a way to integrate that word into their productive language. If students did a collocation pattern search on an English corpus website on *purpose*, they would find that it collocates with *of* most frequently (e.g., *What is the* purpose *of this visit?*). Typically, when discussing collocation patterns, we are concerned with the word(s) used directly to the right of the vocabulary item in question.

Have students make checking collocation patterns of new words part of the routine of learning new words. When introducing new words, draw students' attentions to the words that are used around the new vocabulary item if you recognize that the word has common collocations. Newer dictionaries and learner's dictionaries and online resources often contain this information.

A (10 minutes)

1. Read the directions aloud. Direct students to complete the activity individually.

2. Go over the answers with the class.

> **Activity A Answers, p. 153**
> **1.** tell the truth;
> **2.** tell a lie;
> **3.** tell a story;
> **4.** make a good impression;
> **5.** do the right thing;
> **6.** hurt someone's feelings;
> **7.** get in trouble

B (10 minutes)

Ask for a volunteer to read the directions aloud. Ask students to check their answers with a partner before going over the answers as a class.

> **Activity B Answers, p. 153**
> **1.** truth; **2.** feelings; **3.** the right thing; **4.** stories;
> **5.** trouble; **6.** a good impression

 For additional practice with collocations, have students visit *Q Online Practice.*

WRITING

Writing Skill:
Writing concluding sentences (5 minutes)

1. Ask for volunteers to read aloud. Point out the note about which kind of paragraphs benefit most from concluding sentences.

2. Check comprehension: *What does a good concluding sentence do? What doesn't it do? Do you always need a concluding sentence? Why or why not?*

A (5 minutes)

1. Direct students to read the directions and complete each paragraph. Discuss the example as a class.

2. Have students check their answers with a partner when finished.

> **Activity A Answers, pp. 154–155**
> **1.** c. Only truth can protect the people we love.
> **2.** a. Every day, adults lie to get out of trouble.
> **3.** d. When a person avoids the truth, the person is lying.
> **4.** b. It's OK to tell a lie if it makes someone feel good.

B (10 minutes)

1. Read the directions aloud. Tell students to write sentences to complete the activity.

2. Direct them to discuss their answers with a partner when finished. Ask for volunteers to share their answers with the class.

> **Activity B Answers, p. 155**
> Answers will vary. Possible answers:
> **1.** Honesty is important in relationships between people.;
> **2.** It is important to me to have honest friends like Alex.;
> **3.** Sometimes lies hurt less than the truth.

 For additional practice with writing concluding sentences, have students visit *Q Online Practice.*

Grammar:
Infinitives of purpose (5 minutes)

1. Present information on infinitives of purpose to students. Have students take turns reading aloud the examples. Point out and explain the information in parentheses. Look back at the Unit 2 lesson on infinitives if students need a refresher. Elicit/provide examples of both the infinitive and *in order* + infinitive construction.

2. Do the activity in the following Skill Note.

3. Check comprehension by asking questions: *What is an infinitive? What is an infinitive of purpose? Can you think of an example of an infinitive of purpose that explains why you study English?*

Skill Note

Infinitives of purpose help students expand their ideas and provide clear reasons of support for their main ideas. In the classroom, teachers often ask *Why?* to elicit a longer or more complete response from students—and because users of any language need to be able to explain themselves and their opinions to others.

To practice this skill, ask students a series of *why* questions and have them respond using infinitives of purpose. For example, ask: *Why are you going to school?* (Possible answer: <u>to get</u> a good job.) Ask: *Why do I come to class every day?* (Possible answer: <u>to teach</u> us English.)

MULTILEVEL OPTION

Have higher-level students provide complete sentences as answers (e.g., *You come to class to teach us English*).

Alternatively, pair higher- and lower-level students together and have them write complete sentences as responses to your questions—using infinitives of purpose. Write some of the examples on the board and practice class editing skills.

A (10 minutes)

1. Direct students to read the directions and complete the activity. Reading 1 is on page 144.

2. Put students in pairs to discuss their answers.

3. Call on volunteers to share their ideas with the class.

> **Activity A Answers, p. 156**
> **1.** 8;   **2.** 2

▶ *Reading and Writing 1, page 157*

B (5 minutes)

1. Read the directions aloud. Direct students to complete the activity individually. Read over the example together.

2. Ask for volunteers to share their answers.

> **Activity B Answers, p. 157**
> Answers will vary. Possible answers:
> **1.** to get out of trouble;
> **2.** to make money;
> **3.** in order to protect his friend;
> **4.** to make his friend feel good;
> **5.** in order to hurt his friend

 For additional practice with the infinitives of purpose, have students visit *Q Online Practice*.

Tip for Success (1 minute)

1. Have a volunteer read the tip aloud.

2. Explain to students that using quotation marks to show when someone is speaking is an important skill in academic writing. They will use it more and more as they advance in levels. Quotation marks help writers avoid problems such as plagiarism.

▶ *Reading and Writing 1, page 158*

Unit Assignment:
Write an opinion paragraph

Unit Question (5 minutes)

Refer students back to the ideas they discussed at the beginning of the unit about honesty. Ask the students to retrieve the notes they took from the beginning of this unit when discussing the unit question. Ask students to explain again their answers to the question, *Is it ever OK to lie?* Cue students if necessary by asking specific questions about the content of the unit: *What are some situations in which people tell lies? What are some reasons that adults lie? What are some reasons that children lie?* Read the direction lines for the assignment together to ensure understanding.

Learning Outcome

1. Tie the Unit Assignment to the unit learning outcome. Say: *The outcome for this unit is to write a paragraph that explains your opinion about whether or not it is OK to lie in an online forum. This Unit Assignment is going to let you show your skill at writing paragraphs, using concluding sentences and infinitives of purpose.*

2. Explain that you are going to use a rubric similar to their Self-Assessment checklist on p. 160 to grade their Unit Assignment. You can also share a copy of the Unit Assignment Rubric (on p. 86 of this *Teacher's Handbook*) with the students.

Plan and Write

Brainstorm

A (10 minutes)

1. Read the directions aloud. Put students in pairs to discuss the questions.

Plan

B (10 minutes)

Direct students to complete the planning activity. Remind them that they may use ideas from Activity A or their own.

Tip for Critical Thinking (1 minute)

1. Read the tip aloud.

2. Explain to students that people will better value their opinions and ideas if they are able to justify them with reasons.

Critical Q: Expansion Activity

Justify Your Opinions

1. Write the word *Honesty* on the board. Have each student write one opinion about honesty on a slip of paper.

2. Count students off "1,2,1,2..." until each student in class is either a 1 or a 2. Line the two halves so that they are facing each other (each student should be facing one partner). If there is an odd number of students, you can join in the activity.

3. Have the "1s" read their opinion to their partners. The "2s" then have to justify the opinions of their partners by continuing the sentence with *because*. For example: 1 says, *Honesty is the best policy...*, and 2 continues, *...because lies hurt people.*

4. Once 1 has read his or her opinion and 2 has justified it, 2 should then read his or her opinion and 1 should justify it.

5. Once both partners have read *and* justified each other's opinions, the 1s should take one step to the left (moving in front of a new student) and work with a new partner. The student 1 at the end of the line should go to the other side of the line to find his/her partner.

6. Repeat the activity until all partnership possibilities have been made or until students have had enough practice.

Write

C (10 minutes)

Direct students to write their paragraph in their notebook, referring to the checklist on p. 160.

Your Writing Process (1 minute)

1. Read the Your Writing Process tip aloud.

2. Encourage students to use *Q Online Practice* frequently.

Alternative Unit Assignments

Assign or have students choose one of these assignments to do instead of, or in addition to, the Unit Assignment.

1. Think of a time that you lied. Did you do the right thing? Write a paragraph to explain the situation and why you lied.

2. Read these sayings about honesty. Choose one you agree with. Why do you agree with it? Write a paragraph to explain your reasons.

   a. When you tell the truth, you don't have to remember anything.

   b. A lie may take care of the present, but it has no future.

   c. A half truth is a whole lie.

 For an additional unit assignment, have students visit *Q Online Practice*.

Revise and Edit

Peer Review

A (15–20 minutes)

1. Pair students and direct them to read each other's work.

2. Ask students to answer the questions and discuss them.

3. Give students suggestions of helpful feedback: *Where is your topic sentence? Your concluding sentence was very clear. Try to use some infinitives of purpose to get more practice with them.*

Rewrite

B (15–20 minutes)

Students should review their partners' answers from A and rewrite their paragraphs if necessary.

Edit

C (15–20 minutes)

1. Direct students to read and complete the Self-Assessment checklist. They should be prepared to hand in their work or discuss it in class.

2. Ask for a show of hands for how many students gave all or mostly *Yes* answers.

3. Use the Unit Assignment Rubric on p. 86 in this *Teacher's Handbook* to score each student's assignment.

4. Alternatively, divide the class into large groups and have students read their paragraphs to their group. (Make copies of each student's paragraph for each person in the group, to assist with scoring.) Pass out copies of the Unit Assignment Rubric and have students grade each other.

▶ *Reading and Writing 1, page 161*

Track Your Success (5 minutes)

1. Have students circle the words they have learned in this unit. Suggest that students go back through the unit to review any words they have forgotten.

2. Have students check the skills they have mastered. If students need more practice to feel confident about their proficiency in a skill, point out the pages numbers and encourage them to review.

3. Read the learning outcome aloud (*Write a paragraph that explains your opinion about whether or not it is OK to lie in an online forum*). Ask students if they feel that they have met the outcome.

Unit Assignment Rubric

Student name: _____

Date: _____

Unit Assignment: *Write an opinion paragraph.*

20 = Writing element was completely successful (at least 90% of the time).
15 = Writing element was mostly successful (at least 70% of the time).
10 = Writing element was partially successful (at least 50% of the time).
 0 = Writing element was not successful.

Write an Opinion Paragraph	20 points	15 points	10 points	0 points
Writer uses appropriate subject and object pronouns.				
Student correctly uses collocations and vocabulary from the unit.				
Sentences have both a subject and a verb and those elements agree.				
Infinitives of purpose are correctly used.				
The paragraph has a concluding statement that summarizes the student's opinion about whether or not it is OK to lie in an online forum.				

Total points: _____

Comments:

Unit QUESTION
How are children and adults different?

Life Changes

READING • marking the margins
VOCABULARY • using the dictionary
GRAMMAR • clauses with *after* and *after that*
WRITING • making a timeline to plan your writing

LEARNING OUTCOME

Describe events in your life that made you feel like an adult.

▶ *Reading and Writing 1, page 163*

Preview the Unit

Learning Outcome

1. Ask for a volunteer to read the unit skills, then the unit learning outcome.

2. Explain: *This is what you are expected to be able to do by the unit's end. The learning outcome explains how you are going to be evaluated. With this outcome in mind, you should focus on learning these skills (Reading, Vocabulary, Writing, Grammar) that will support your goal of describing events in your life that made you feel like an adult. This can also help you act as mentors in the classroom to help the other students meet this outcome.*

A (10 minutes)

1. Elicit adults' responsibilities and children's responsibilities and write them on the board. Alternatively, have students write the responsibilities on the board themselves.

2. Put students in pairs or small groups to discuss the first two questions.

3. Call on volunteers to share their ideas with the class. Ask questions: *Why do adults have different responsibilities than children?*

4. Focus students' attention on the photo. Have a volunteer describe the photo to the class. Read the final question aloud. Have students raise their hands if they think they are children and tally the answers. Then have students raise their hands if they think they are adults and tally the answers.

5. Pair students together who had opposite answers and have them explain to each other why they chose their answer. Ask: *What actions in the photo made you choose your answer?*

Activity A Answers, p. 163
Answers will vary. Possible answers:
1. Yes, I support myself and live on my own. No, I am still considered a minor in my country.
2. Ages when people are considered adults vary.
3. The woman is driving. The girl is sitting. They are driving to the store. The girl is a child and the driver is an adult.

B (5 minutes)

1. Introduce the Unit Question, *How are children and adults different?* Ask related information questions or questions about personal experience to help students prepare for answering the more abstract Unit Question. Ask: *How are your parents different from you? If you have children, how are your children different from you?*

2. Tell the students: *Let's start off our discussion by listing differences between children and adults. For example, we could start our list with* work *because many adults have jobs and many children do not. But there are many other differences. What else can we think of?*

3. Seat students in small groups and direct them to pass around a paper as quickly as they can, with each group member adding one item to the list. Tell them they have two minutes to make the lists and they should write as many words as possible.

4. Call time and ask a reporter from each group to read the list aloud.

5. Use items from the list as a springboard for discussion. For example: *From our lists, we see that children often go to school and adults sometimes do not. What makes some adults want to go back to school? Also, we see that adults pay bills and children often do not. When do children help pay bills?*

Activity B Answers, p. 163

Answers will vary. Possible answers: Adults have jobs. Children go to school. Children are young, and adults are not.

The Q Classroom (5 minutes)

CD2, Track 11

1. Play The Q Classroom. Use the example from the audio to help students continue the conversation. Ask: *How did the students answer the question? What do you think about their ideas?*

2. Felix says that children learn more easily, but adults understand things better. Ask: *Why do you think Felix has these opinions? Do you agree with him? Why or why not?*

▶ *Reading and Writing 1, page 164*

C (10 minutes)

Ask a volunteer to read the directions aloud. Remind students that they should complete the survey individually and then discuss their results with a small group once everyone has finished. The group should tally the total number of Yes's and No's for each statement.

D (10 minutes)

1. Read the directions aloud. Model the activity by providing an example answer (e.g., *These photos don't change my idea of an adult because I am confident I know what an adult is like.*).

2. Ask students to write their answers down individually. Then have them share their answers with their group members.

3. Walk around the room and listen to answers. Select a few model answers and ask those students to share their thoughts with the entire class after all groups have finished their conversations.

EXPANSION ACTIVITY: The Best Thing? (15 minutes)

1. Have adult students think of the best thing about being a child. Have young students think about the best thing about being an adult.

2. Pair students up according to their focus ("child" with "child" and "adult" with "adult") and have them share their answers.

3. Place pairs into larger groups, according to their focus, and have them share their answers again.

4. Have students share answers with the class while you write some of them on the board. Ask: *Why is (insert answer) the best thing about being a child (adult)?*

5. If you have both children and adults in the classroom, have them comment on the answers. Ask: *Is (insert answer) really the best thing about being a child (adult)?*

▶ *Reading and Writing 1, page 165*

READING

READING 1: What Is an Adult?

VOCABULARY (10 minutes)

1. Ask volunteers to read each of the vocabulary items plus their definitions. Model pronunciation as necessary.

2. After students read the definitions, have students in pairs try to place each vocabulary item into sentences 1–9. Ask students to cross out used vocabulary items as they fill in the sentences.

3. Group pairs into larger groups and have students check and correct answers.

4. Correct answers as a class.

MULTILEVEL OPTION

Place students in mixed-ability pairs. The higher-level students can assist lower-level students in filling in the blanks and explain their understanding of the meaning of the words. Direct students to alternate reading the sentences aloud. Encourage them to help each other with pronunciation.

Alternatively, have higher-level students write an additional sample sentence for each expression. Have volunteers share their sentences with the class by giving their sentence to a lower-level student to write on the board. Correct the sentences with the whole class, focusing on the use of the expression rather than other grammatical issues.

Vocabulary Answers, p. 165

1. responsibility; **2.** organize; **3.** judgment;
4. grown; **5.** vote; **6.** legal;
7. permission; **8.** define; **9.** right

 For additional practice with the vocabulary, have students visit *Q Online Practice.*

▶ *Reading and Writing 1, page 166*

Reading Skill:
Marking the margins (10 minutes)

1. Introduce this reading skill. Point out the margins on the page of the student book. The outside margins usually have more room to write in, but it is clearer to mark the margin on the left side of the page.

2. Check comprehension by asking questions: *Why do people mark the margins of readings? What symbols can we use to mark the margins? What does each symbol mean?*

A (10 minutes)

1. Ask a volunteer to read the directions. To check their understanding, ask the class: *What do you need to do now?*

2. Have students complete the task. Circulate and answer questions as needed.

3. Have students compare answers with a partner. Then check answers as a class.

4. Do the activity in the following Skill Note (below B) with your class.

> **Reading Skill A Answers, p. 166**
> **1.** *Rumspringa*;
> **2.** They don't use cars, TVs, or most kinds of technology.;
> **3.** Children need to make their own decision.

B (5 minutes)

1. Have a volunteer read the directions. Remind them that they will do this as they read the reading in the next section.

2. Model marking the margins by reviewing the four symbols—?/!/√/×—and eliciting what those symbols signify.

> **Reading Skill B Answers, p. 166**
> Answers will vary.

 For additional practice with marking the margins, have students visit *Q Online Practice*.

Skill Note

Marking the margins of a reading is a crucial tool for becoming an efficient reader. Instead of taking 5–10 minutes to process simple underlining or highlighting, the use of symbols helps students quickly understand how he or she felt about particular words, phrases, or sentences in a reading. The reader knows immediately if he or she needs to look up a word in a dictionary or use a sentence in a class discussion as a point of agreement or disagreement, depending on the symbol he or she marked in the margin. Readers can quickly access important information by scanning to find the symbol they want in that moment.

Practice this skill by having students turn to a previous reading in the student book. Give students 3–5 minutes to skim the text and mark the margins with appropriate symbols. Then pair students and have them trade books. Partners should easily be able to interpret their partner's symbols. Ask: *What did your partner find interesting? Confusing? What did your partner agree with? Disagree with?*

▶ *Reading and Writing 1, page 167*

PREVIEW READING 1 (5 minutes)

1. Direct students to read and complete the activity.

2. Tell students they should review their answer with a partner after reading.

> **Preview Reading 1 Answer, p. 167**
> to show the part of the brain that controls much adult thinking

Reading 1 Background Note

Age is an important issue for people. Young people often want to appear older. Child actors such as Miley Cyrus and Daniel Radcliffe have looked for roles that would make people think of them as older. On the other hand, older people often want to appear younger. On TV and in magazines, one can find products that appeal to older people by marketing their "age-defying" effects that erase wrinkles. There are also products marketed to young people with slogans such as "act like an adult" or "be like Mom!" Such products, and a focus on appearing to be younger or older, have prompted some people to ask: What's wrong with being your own age? What's wrong with being yourself?

READ

 CD2, Track 12

1. Instruct students to read the excerpt *What Is an Adult?*

2. Play the audio and have students follow along.

MAIN IDEAS (10 minutes)

1. Preview the statements with students and ensure they understand the vocabulary.

2. Ask students to read and complete the activity on their own.

3. Read the statements. Have students raise their left hands for false and their right hands for true. Provide or confirm correct answers. Check for understanding.

Main Idea Answers, p. 168
1. F; **2.** F; **3.** T; **4.** T

DETAILS (15 minutes)

1. Direct students to read the statements and complete the activity.

2. Have students compare answers with a partner.

3. Direct the students to look back at the article to check their answers.

4. Go over the answers with the class.

Details Answers, pp. 168–169
1. c; **2.** a; **3.** a; **4.** c; **5.** b; **6.** a

 For additional practice with reading comprehension, have students visit *Q Online Practice*.

▶ *Reading and Writing 1, page 169*

WHAT DO YOU THINK? (20 minutes)

1. Ask students to read the statements and reflect on their answers.

2. Seat students in small groups and assign roles: a group leader to make sure everyone contributes, a note-taker to record the group's ideas, a reporter to share the group's ideas with the class, and a timekeeper to watch the clock.

3. Give students five minutes to discuss the statements. Call time if conversations are winding down. Allow extra time if necessary.

4. Call on each group's reporter to share ideas with the class.

5. Have each student choose one of the questions to write a paragraph response.

6. Call on volunteers to share ideas with the class.

What Do You Think? Answers, p. 169
Answers will vary. Possible answers:
1. I marked the idea that the brain grows until a person is 25 as interesting because I never knew that.
2. I disagreed with the idea that an adult is someone who can have children. I know someone who is young and has a child; however, I do not think of her as an adult.
3. I didn't understand the idea that in India, a man can't marry until he is 21 without his parents' permission. Can you explain that to me?

Learning Outcome

Use the learning outcome to frame the purpose and relevance of Reading 1. Ask: *What did you learn from Reading 1 that prepares you to describe events from your life that made you feel like an adult?*

▶ *Reading and Writing 1, page 170*

READING 2: Becoming an Adult

VOCABULARY (20 minutes)

1. Ask for a volunteer to read the heading and directions aloud. Check students' understanding by asking them what they need to do (read the sentences and write the bold words next to their definitions).

2. Check answers as a class. Write each bolded vocabulary word on a separate sheet of paper. Distribute each sheet of paper to one of nine volunteers and ask them to sit/crouch in front of the class.

3. As the class provides a vocabulary word for each blank, have the volunteer who is holding that vocabulary word stand up and repeat the word. Ensure that the selected word and its pronunciation is correct.

4. Call on a volunteer to read the entire sentence aloud.

Vocabulary Answers, p. 170

a. burn

b. celebration

c. century

d. collect

e. participate

f. ceremony

g. village

h. chase

i. represent

 For additional practice with the vocabulary, have students visit *Q Online Practice*.

MULTILEVEL OPTION

Have higher-level students think of new sentences in which to use the new vocabulary items.

Have lower-level students write selected sentences on the board for the class to read.

Alternatively, have higher-level students write sentences with two or three vocabulary words in each one, while lower-level students write sentences with one of the vocabulary words.

▶ *Reading and Writing 1, page 171*

PREVIEW READING 2 (5 minutes)

1. Read the directions aloud to the class. Remind them what they've learned about scanning in previous units. Ask if they remember/know what a *blog* is.

2. Have students complete the activity.

3. Have students review their answers after scanning.

> **Preview Reading 2 Answers, p. 171**
> Astrid: Norway; Yasa: Papua New Guinea; Min Joo: Korea

Reading 2 Background Note

The term *rites of passage* is another phrase for *coming-of-age event*. Rites of passage are traditional events that mark the transition from childhood to adulthood. In some corners of the world, people are sent on hunting trips to prove they are ready for adulthood. In other corners, people are asked to isolate themselves from their society for a time, only coming back when some task has been completed. While the details differ, the result is the same—when you finish the rite, you are an adult. Why do your students think that such rites exist?

READ

 CD2, Track 13

1. Instruct students to read the *Becoming an Adult* blog postings.

2. Play the audio and have students follow along.

▶ *Reading and Writing 1, page 173*

MAIN IDEAS (5 minutes)

1. Choose a student to read the directions aloud.

2. Ask students to read and complete the activity individually.

3. Check answers as a class and discuss their reasoning.

> **Main Idea Answers, p. 173**
> **1.** N; **2.** P; **3.** P; **4.** K; **5.** N **6.** K

DETAILS (10 minutes)

1. Direct students to read the statements and complete the activity.

2. Have students compare answers with a partner.

3. Direct the students to look back at the article to check their answers.

4. Go over the answers with the class.

> **Details Answers, p. 173**
> **1.** c; **2.** a; **3.** b; **4.** c; **5.** b; **6.** b

 For additional practice with reading comprehension, have students visit *Q Online Practice*.

▶ *Reading and Writing 1, page 174*

WHAT DO YOU THINK?

A (10 minutes)

1. Ask students to read the questions and reflect on their answers.

2. Seat students in small groups and assign roles: a group leader to make sure everyone contributes, a note-taker to record the group's ideas, a reporter to share the group's ideas with the class, and a timekeeper to watch the clock.

3. Give students five minutes to discuss the questions. Call time if conversations are winding down. Allow them an extra minute or two if necessary.

Activity A Answers, p. 174

1. Answers will vary. Possible answers: An adult is someone who works. An adult is someone who has kids.

2. Answers will vary.

MULTILEVEL OPTION

Have lower-level students pair with higher-level students to write a few sentences about ceremonies in their cultures. Higher-level students should write what the lower-level students say about ceremonies in their cultures (two or three sentences).

B (10 minutes)

1. Tell the students that they should think about both Reading 1 and Reading 2 as they answer the questions in B. Have them go back and reread Reading 1 if needed.

2. Ask students to discuss their answers with a partner.

3. Call on each pair to share ideas with the class.

Activity B Answers, p. 174

1. Yes, I think some people become adults before others. No, I don't agree.

2. Answers will vary.

Learning Outcome

Use the learning outcome to frame the purpose and relevance of Readings 1 and 2. Ask: *What did you learn from Reading 2 that prepares you to describe events from your life that made you feel like an adult?*

▶ *Reading and Writing 1, page 175*

Vocabulary Skill: Using the dictionary (15 minutes)

1. Ask students: *When a word in the dictionary has many definitions, how do you know which one to use?* Have a volunteer read the explanation of this vocabulary skill to the class. Go over the example together.

2. Check comprehension: *What are two ways to figure out which is the correct definition to use? How can these two methods help you figure out the definition of the word?*

3. Model the activity by completing Activity A, Statement 1 together as a class.

Skill Note

Context provides many clues as to the meanings of words. Paul Nation, an applied linguistics professor at Victoria University of Wellington, New Zealand, notes that to know a word means that in addition to knowing a word's definition, one must know how to use the word correctly and recognize its meaning in context. Online corpora and learner's dictionaries allow teachers and students quick access to similar words used in different parts of speech—thereby allowing them to see how new vocabulary items are used in different contexts and helping them induce the definition from multiple examples.

Call up an online corpus in class, such as the American Corpus provided by Brigham Young University, and type in a vocabulary word from this unit (e.g., *represent* or *collect*). Read through some of the examples sentences that pop up and elicit patterns of usage for that particular word—collect *in*, collect *on*, or collect *from*. From these contexts, ask students to recall the definitions of these words. Encourage students to continue to use contextual clues to learn what words mean and how to use them.

A (15 minutes)

1. Have students work individually to complete the activity. Pair students to compare answers.

2. Go over the answers with the class. Elicit example sentences using some of the bolded vocabulary items.

Activity A Answers, pp. 175–176

1. 2; **2.** 1; **3.** 1; **4.** 3; **5.** 2; **6.** 2; **7.** 1

▶ *Reading and Writing 1, page 176*

B (10 minutes)

1. Direct students to read the sentences, look the bolded vocabulary items in the dictionary, and write the correct definition. Make sure there are enough dictionaries in the class for everyone.

2. Have students share answers in pairs. Then share answers with the entire class.

Activity B Answers, p. 176

Answers will vary. Possible answers:

1. right: morally good, justified, or acceptable;

2. represent: be a spokesperson for;

3. judgment: an opinion formed by making your mind up about something

 For additional practice with using the dictionary, have students visit *Q Online Practice*.

WRITING

▶ Reading and Writing 1, page 177

Grammar: Clauses with *after* and *after that* (10 minutes)

1. Have students read the first paragraph of the explanation of *after* clauses. Write on the board or point out the example sentence for *after* clauses. Have students explain how they know one event (getting a job) comes before the other event (moving out of the parents' house).

2. Have students read the first paragraph of the explanation of *after that* clauses. Write the example sentence for *after that* clauses on the board. Have students explain how they know one event (getting a license) comes before the other event (feeling like an adult).

3. Point out that sentence order can change depending on where you place *after* or *after that* (i.e., the first event can occur last in the sentence). However, if *after that* comes at the beginning of a sentence, a comma needs to immediately follow it.

4. Check comprehension: *What is the difference between a clause that begins with* after *and* after that? *Can you think of a sentence that begins with* after? *If I give you the sentence:* I graduated from high school in May, *can you give me a sentence that begins with* after that? Correct sentences as needed.

A (10 minutes)

1. Direct students to read the directions for the activity.

2. Have them complete the activity in pairs.

3. Go over the answers with the class.

> **Activity A Answers, p. 177**
> 1. Circle: I turned 18,
>   Underline: I graduated from high school;
> 2. Circle: I finished college,
>   Underline: I moved to New York;
> 3. Circle: I had my first child when I was 25,
>   Underline: I wanted another child;
> 4. Circle: the coming-of-age ceremony,
>   Underline: my friends and I went to a party;
> 5. Circle: I voted for the first time,
>   Underline: I felt like a responsible adult;
> 6. Circle: I turned 18, Underline: I learned how to drive.

▶ Reading and Writing 1, page 178

B (10 minutes)

1. Direct students to read the directions for the activity.

2. Have them complete the activity individually.

3. Go over the answers with the class.

> **Activity B Answers, p. 178**
> 1. After we got married, my wife and I moved to California.;
> 2. After I went to my coming-of-age ceremony, I still didn't feel like an adult.;
> 3. I moved out of my parents' house when I was 19. After that, I had a difficult time.
> 4. I turned 16 last year. After that, I started being more responsible.

 For additional practice with clauses with *after* and *after that*, have students visit *Q Online Practice*.

Writing Skill: Making a timeline to plan your writing (15 minutes)

1. Ask students: *What is a timeline? Have you ever seen a timeline before? When? How was it used?* Have a volunteer read the first paragraph of the explanation to the class.

2. Go over the timeline with the students. Then draw a blank timeline on the board and fill in your day. Before you fill it in, have students try to guess various events that occurred in your day. Compare your timeline to the one in the book.

3. Do the activity in the following Skill Note with your class.

4. Check comprehension by asking questions: *What happens at the left side of a timeline?* (The first action) *What happens at the right side of a timeline?* (The last action) *What can a timeline help you write?* (A narrative or a story) *Should a paragraph only have information from the timeline?* (No, a timeline can have other details as well.)

Skill Note

Outlining ideas before beginning a writing assignment is a good way for a writer to figure out what he or she wants to communicate. When writing a paragraph detailing the writer's day, a timeline is a quick and efficient way to brainstorm ideas for that paragraph. Getting ideas out before committing to the larger writing task helps writers make connections among their ideas and decide how they want to present them to the reader. It also helps lower-level writers realize that they know more than they think they know!

Remind students that timelines can deal with a short period of time—like a day—or a long period of time—like months or years. Many successful people use timelines to visualize what they want to accomplish during a certain period of time. For example, some people create a 10-year plan where they lay out what they want to accomplish during those 10 years.

Tip for Critical Thinking (1 minute)

1. Read the tip aloud.
2. Point out to students that it's often a good idea to think creatively when constructing something new.

Critical Q: Expansion Activity

Reconstructing Rules

1. Elicit from students rules that their parents had (have) for them as children. Have each student write these rules on a piece of paper. Ask: *How did you feel about these rules? Did you think they were fair or unfair? Why?*
2. Have students imagine those rules as if they were providing them for their own children. Have each student write these rules on a piece of paper. Ask: *How would the rules be the same? How would they be different? Why?*
3. Have volunteers read example rules from their childhoods and equivalent example rules they would give/have given as parents. Encourage students to discuss the similarities and differences between the sets of rules. Ask: *In creating the new sets of rules for your children, why were some rules similar? Why were some rules different?*
4. Ask: *Why is it important for parents to provide rules for their children?*

▶ *Reading and Writing 1, page 179*

A (10 minutes)

1. Direct students to make a timeline of their perfect day.
2. Put students in pairs to share the events that happened during their perfect day.
3. Call on volunteers to share their days' events with the class.

B (15 minutes)

1. Direct students to complete the activity individually, sharing their sentences with a partner once done.
2. Have pairs summarize their partners' days aloud for the class.

21ST CENTURY SKILLS

To visualize and articulate the connection between past events and their effect on the transition to adulthood, help students include "cause and effect" type argumentation into their active critical thinking processes.

To do this, ask students to think about important events in their lives: graduations, marriages, employment, successes, and failures (note that learning from mistakes is also an important 21st century skill). When students have selected an event, have them create a **timeline**, like they did earlier, showing all of the "small" events that led up to that "large" event. Individually, have students write a paragraph that explains how those "small" events allowed that "large" event to occur. Have students then share their stories in pairs and with the class. Encourage students to always look for, and be able to discuss, connections between past and present events.

Unit Assignment: Write one or two paragraphs about events in your life

Unit Question (5 minutes)

Refer students back to the ideas they discussed at the beginning of the unit about events in their lives that made them feel like adults. Remind them of traditions that different cultures have in relation to "coming-of-age." Cue students if necessary by asking specific questions about the content of the unit: *What are differences between children and adults? How do some cultures show when a child has become an adult? What types of "coming-of-age" traditions do you have in your culture?* Read the direction lines for the assignment together to ensure understanding.

Learning Outcome

1. Tie the Unit Assignment to the unit learning outcome. Say: *The outcome for this unit is to describe events in your lives that made you feel like an adult. This Unit Assignment is going to let you show your skill in writing one or two paragraphs about these events. Explaining the events in your lives that made you who you are practices making connections between causes and effects.*

2. Explain that you are going to use a rubric similar to their Self-Assessment checklist on p. 180 to grade their Unit Assignment. You can also share a copy of the Unit Assignment Rubric (on p. 97 of this *Teacher's Handbook*) with the students.

Plan and Write

Brainstorm

A (10 minutes)

Direct students to complete Activity A and share answers with a partner.

Plan

B (15 minutes)

1. Have students complete the timelines individually.

2. Pair students and have them share the events of their days.

3. Circulate around the room, providing help and answering questions as needed.

Tip for Success (1 minute)

1. Read the tip to students.

2. Provide a model paragraph for your students to work from. For example: *I feel like an adult because I have bills to pay. I have to make sure that my electricity stays on. I have to make payments on my car, and I have to pay my rent. All of these bills remind me that I am adult with adult responsibilities.*

▶ *Reading and Writing 1, page 180*

Write

C (20 minutes)

1. Go over the directions.

2. Remind students to use vocabulary items from the unit where possible and *after* and *after that* clauses. Review the vocabulary and *after* and *after that* clauses if you feel students need a review.

3. If appropriate, give students a specific number and/or a list of vocabulary items they must use.

Alternative Unit Assignments

Assign or have students choose one of these assignments to do instead of, or in addition to, the Unit Assignment.

1. How is your life different now than it was 10 years ago? Write a paragraph about 3–5 important changes in your life in the past 10 years.

2. Imagine that you are applying for a job. Write a paragraph describing several of your past achievements.

 For an additional unit assignment, have students visit *Q Online Practice.*

Revise and Edit

Peer Review

A (15–20 minutes)

1. Pair students and direct them to read each other's work.

2. Ask students to answer the questions and discuss them.

3. Give students suggestions of helpful feedback: *I liked your writing because…. Can you be clearer about what events made you an adult? I don't see an example of* after/after that.

Rewrite

B (15–20 minutes)

Students should review their partners' answers from A and rewrite their paragraphs if necessary.

C (15–20 minutes)

1. Direct students to read and complete the Self-Assessment checklist. They should be prepared to hand in their work or discuss it in class.

2. Ask for a show of hands for how many students gave all or mostly *yes* answers.

3. Use the Unit Assignment Rubric on p. 97 in this *Teacher's Handbook* to score each student's assignment.

4. Alternatively, divide the class into large groups and have students read their paragraphs to their group. (Make copies of each student's writing for each person in the group, to assist with scoring.) Pass out copies of the Unit Assignment Rubric and have students grade each other.

▶ *Reading and Writing 1, page 181*

Track Your Success (5 minutes)

1. Have students circle the words they have learned in this unit. Suggest that students go back through the unit to review any words they have forgotten.

2. Have students check the skills they have mastered. If students need more practice to feel confident about their proficiency in a skill, point out the pages numbers and encourage them to review.

3. Read the learning outcome aloud (*Describe events in your life that made you feel like an adult*). Ask students if they feel that they have met the outcome.

Unit Assignment Rubric

Student name: _____

Date: _____

Unit Assignment: *Write one or two paragraphs about events in your life.*

20 = Writing element was completely successful (at least 90% of the time).
15 = Writing element was mostly successful (at least 70% of the time).
10 = Writing element was partially successful (at least 50% of the time).
 0 = Writing element was not successful.

Writing One or Two Paragraphs	20 points	15 points	10 points	0 points
Student is able to describe 4–6 events that made him/her feel like an adult.				
Sentences have both a subject and a verb and those elements agree.				
The first line of each paragraph is indented, and sentences begin with capital letters and end with appropriate punctuation.				
After and *after that* clauses are correctly used.				
The writer uses correct spelling and a good variety of vocabulary words from this unit.				

Total points: _____

Comments:

| READING • identifying facts and opinions |
| VOCABULARY • word families |
| WRITING • contrasting ideas with *however* |
| GRAMMAR • comparative adjectives |

LEARNING OUTCOME

Describe an unreasonable fear and explain how it can be avoided.

▶ *Reading and Writing 1, page 183*

Preview the Unit

Learning Outcome

1. Ask for a volunteer to read the unit skills, then the unit learning outcome.

2. Explain: *This is what you are expected to be able to do by the unit's end. The learning outcome explains how you are going to be evaluated. With this outcome in mind, you should focus on learning these skills (Reading, Vocabulary, Writing, Grammar) that will support your goal of describing an unreasonable fear and explaining how it can be avoided. This can also help you act as mentors in the classroom to help the other students meet this outcome.*

A (10 minutes)

1. Write the word *fear* on the board. Ask students: *What do you think about when you see the word* fear? *What makes people fear something, or feel afraid? How do people feel when they are afraid? Do people like to feel afraid? Why or why not?*

2. Put students in pairs or small groups to discuss the first two questions in A.

3. Call on volunteers to share their ideas with the class. Ask questions: *What do you do when you feel afraid? What do you think about when you feel afraid? What do you think about people who say they are never afraid of anything? What do you think of people who say they are afraid of many things?*

4. Focus students' attention on the photo. Have a volunteer describe the photo to the class. Read the third question aloud. Ask questions: *What parts of this picture make people feel afraid? What does this picture make you feel? Why do you think people are so afraid of spiders?*

Activity A Answers, p. 183
Answers will vary. Possible answers:
1. Yes, I easily become afraid. No, I don't easily become afraid.
2. I stay safe by paying attention to things around me. I don't go out when it is dark.
3. Yes, I am afraid of spiders. No, I am not afraid of spiders.

B (10 minutes)

1. Introduce the Unit Question, *What are you afraid of?* Ask: *What is your first memory of being afraid? What do you do when you feel afraid? If someone you know feels afraid, how can you help? Do you think fear can be a good thing? Why or why not?*

2. Label four pieces of poster paper with four interesting answers to the question above, *What are you afraid of?* (e.g., insects, making mistakes, heights, or other) and place them in the corners of the room.

3. Ask students to read and consider the unit question for a moment and then to stand in the corner next to the poster that best represents their answer to the question. If the students stand by only one or two answers, have them select a second choice to spread the students out a little.

4. Direct the groups in each corner to talk among themselves about the reasons for their answers. Tell them to choose a note-taker to record the answers on the poster paper.

5. Call on volunteers from each corner to share their opinions with the class.

6. Keep the posters for students to refer back to at the end of the unit.

Activity B Answers, p. 183
Answers will vary. Possible answers: I am afraid of insects. Walking alone at night makes me feel afraid. I am afraid of losing my job.

The Q Classroom (5 minutes)

CD2, Track 14

1. Play The Q Classroom. Use the example from the audio to help students continue the conversation. Ask: *How did the students answer the question? Do you agree or disagree with their ideas? Why?*

2. On the audio, the teacher says that fear is not always logical. Elicit reasons why students might agree or disagree with the teacher's statement. Ask: *What does* logical *mean? Why do you think the teacher believes fear sometimes isn't logical? Do you have logical fears? Illogical fears? What are they?*

▶ *Reading and Writing 1, page 184*

C (10 minutes)

1. Ask for a volunteer to read the directions. Model the first statement in front of the class by drawing a line on the board similar to the one in this exercise. Have volunteers place their X on the part of the line that matches how they feel. Ask: *Why do you strongly agree/disagree?*

2. Have students complete the activity individually. Then have students share their answers with a partner when finished. Have students defend their choices.

D (5 minutes)

1. Ask a volunteer to read the directions aloud. Have students write their answers in their notebooks.

2. Group students together and have them discuss their responses to the questions.

EXPANSION ACTIVITY: What Would You Do? (20 minutes)

1. Ask students to brainstorm a list of 10 things that scare them. Write these items on the board or have a student write them on the board. Items might include strangers, dogs, cars, knives, loud noises, etc.

2. Have students divide a sheet of paper into three columns. Have students choose one item to put at the top of each column. Since there are three columns, students will choose three items.

3. Tell students that they are going to go around the room and ask each other if they are afraid of the items they chose. For example, a student might ask, *Are you afraid of dogs?* (Any item from the list on the board can be substituted for the underlined word.) If a student replies, *No,* then the student has to keep asking other students until they get a *yes.*

4. When students receive a *yes* answer, they have to write that student's name on their paper. Then they have to ask, *What do you do when you see dogs?* (Any item from the list on the board can be substituted for the underlined word.) Have students write down their partner's answer.

5. Once each, or most, students get one answer for each item, they can sit down and share answers with other students who have finished.

6. Share answers with the class.

MULTILEVEL OPTION

Pair lower- and higher-level students. Have the lower-level student be the interviewer and the higher-level student be the writer. Conduct the *What Would You Do?* activity as described above, completing it in pairs instead of individually.

READING

▶ *Reading and Writing 1, page 185*

READING 1: A Dangerous World?

Tip for Success (1 minute)

Read the tip aloud. Explain to students that confusing *affect* and *effect* is a common error—not just for students learning English but for native speakers as well!

VOCABULARY (10 minutes)

1. Read the heading and directions. Ask students to work individually to match vocabulary words with answers.

2. Put students in pairs to compare answers. Elicit the answers from volunteers. Have students repeat the bolded vocabulary words.

3. Ask questions to help students connect with the vocabulary: *What other things can* **affect** *your health? Why do people like* **scary** *movies? What is a* **common** *way to avoid things that scare you?*

> **Vocabulary Answers, p. 185**
> **a.** negative; **b.** scary; **c.** crime; **d.** focus;
> **e.** violent; **f.** common; **g.** affect; **h.** report

 For additional practice with the vocabulary, have students visit *Q Online Practice.*

 Reading and Writing 1, page 186

PREVIEW READING 1 (5 minutes)

1. Direct students to read the directions individually and complete the activity.

2. Tell students they should review their answer after reading.

> **Preview Reading 1 Answer, p. 186**
> It's gone down.

Reading 1 Background Note

Television is one of the most popular ways that people get their news. In the early days of TV, a TV anchor (a person on TV who reads the news) would explain the day's events to viewers. That formula changed in 1980 when Ted Turner launched the Cable News Network (CNN) in the United States. CNN invented the 24-hour news cycle, which meant that every hour of every day of the year, producers had to find news to put on TV. Now, many more 24-hour news networks exist.

No news network wants to be beaten to a story by a competitor, so many stories are continually updated to make sure that viewers won't switch to another network. So if there is a violent news story, a news network might show the same violent images over and over during the course of a day. These repeated violent images can affect the viewers' sense of how violent the world is. In fact, any topic repeated over and over during a news cycle can distort a viewer's idea of how common such images are in the real world.

READ

 CD2, Track 15

1. Instruct students to read the article.

2. Play the audio and have students follow along.

Reading and Writing 1, page 187

MAIN IDEAS (5 minutes)

1. Tell students that if they are truly skimming, not reading, they should be able to answer the questions quickly.

2. Ask students to read and complete the activity individually.

3. Ask volunteers to share their answers. Check understanding by having students look back at the reading to confirm their answers.

> **Main Idea Answers, p. 187**
> **1.** b; **2.** a; **3.** a; **4.** b

Reading and Writing 1, page 188

DETAILS (5 minutes)

1. Direct students to circle the best answers to complete the activity.

2. Have students compare answers with a partner.

3. Direct the students to look back at the article to check their answers.

4. Go over the answers with the class.

> **Details Answers, p. 188**
> **1.** b; **2.** a; **3.** b; **4.** c; **5.** a

 For additional practice with reading comprehension, have students visit *Q Online Practice.*

> **MULTILEVEL OPTION**
>
> Place students in mixed-ability pairs. Have students go back to the reading and find the bolded vocabulary items from p. 185. Then have pairs come up with another sentence for each bolded word. Check sentences in small groups and write model sentences on the board.

WHAT DO YOU THINK? (20 minutes)

1. Ask students to read the questions and reflect on their answers.

2. Seat students in small groups and assign roles: a group leader to make sure everyone contributes, a note-taker to record the group's ideas, a reporter to share the group's ideas with the class, and a timekeeper to watch the clock.

3. Give students five minutes to discuss the questions. Call time if conversations are winding down. Allow them an extra minute or two if necessary.

4. Call on each group's reporter to share ideas with the class.

5. Have each student choose one of the questions and write two or three sentences in response.

6. Call on volunteers to share their ideas with the class.

> **MULTILEVEL OPTION**
>
> Have higher-level students write more sentences. Alternatively, places students in mixed-ability pairs and choose a higher-level student from each group to lead the discussion of questions 1–3.

What Do You Think? Answers, p. 188
Answers will vary.

Learning Outcome

Use the learning outcome to frame the purpose and relevance of Reading 1. Ask: *What did you learn from Reading 1 that prepares you to describe an unreasonable fear and explain how it can be avoided?*

▶ *Reading and Writing 1, page 189*

Reading Skill:
Identifying facts and opinions (10 minutes)

1. Go over the presentation for this skill. Elicit examples of facts and opinions, making sure the verbs *think* and *believe* are used.

2. Check comprehension by asking questions: *What is a fact? What is an opinion? When during your day do you hear facts? When do you hear opinions? Why is it important to be able to tell the difference between facts and opinions? What words can help you tell the difference between facts and opinions? How will this skill be helpful for you as a student?*

 For additional practice with identifying facts and opinions, have students visit *Q Online Practice*.

Skill Note

When writing academic research papers, students must be able to tell the difference between facts and opinions. Facts support arguments. Opinions provide interesting details; however, they might not persuade a reader of the writer's argument. Academic writing, which is often about presenting an argument to inform or persuade, weakens when the writer confuses facts and opinions. Thus, students benefit from an early and sustained effort to help them see linguistic differences between the ways facts and opinions are presented.

A (10 minutes)

1. Have a volunteer read the directions for the activity. Complete item 1 as a class. Elicit rationale for answers.

2. Direct students to complete the remaining sentences individually and compare their answers with a partner.

3. Go over the answers with the class. Elicit corrections as necessary.

Activity A Answers, p. 189
1. a-F, b-O;   **2.** a-O, b-F;   **3.** a-O, b-F;   **4.** a-F, b-O

B (5 minutes)

1. Ask for a volunteer to read the directions.

2. Have students complete the task individually and share answers with a partner.

3. Check answers as a class and remind students of the vocabulary that signals a fact and the vocabulary that signals an opinion.

Activity B Answers, p. 189
*However, most people **believe** that crime rates are increasing; They **think** that violent crime happens in their towns and cities all the time; People **believe** there is more crime than there really is; They **think** violent crime is common; They **believe** the world outside is too dangerous; Television's focus on crime makes us **believe** the world is a scarier place than it is. It's good to be careful and stay safe, but the world around us is actually safer than we **think**.*

▶ *Reading and Writing 1, page 190*

READING 2: Can We Trust Our Fears?

VOCABULARY (20 minutes)

1. Read the directions and check students' understanding by asking them what they need to do to complete the activity.

2. Go over the bolded words and definitions. Check pronunciation as necessary.

3. Ask for volunteers to give their answers and check to see that everyone agrees.

4. Once students have worked with the new vocabulary items a little bit, ask students to write a paragraph about their own fears. Have each student use two or three of the new vocabulary items in their paragraphs.

Vocabulary Answers, p. 193

1. harm; **2.** factor; **3.** death;
4. reasonable; **5.** frighten; **6.** fat;
7. disease; **8.** pleasure; **9.** contain

 For additional practice with the vocabulary, have students visit *Q Online Practice*.

MULTILEVEL OPTION

Have lower-level students write fewer sentences, or sentences that contain just one of the vocabulary words.

Have higher-level students write more by expanding upon their answers with specific details.

▶ *Reading and Writing 1, page 191*

PREVIEW READING 2 (5 minutes)

1. Read the directions aloud.

2. Place students into mixed-ability pairs and have them discuss the question.

3. Tell students they should review their answer after reading.

Reading 2 Background Note

U.S. President Franklin Delano Roosevelt said that people have nothing to fear but fear itself. It is the fear of something happening rather than the thing itself that often paralyzes people. A recent *Newsweek* article, however, questions whether people are afraid of the correct things. The article uses statistics to show that the things people really are afraid of have a much *lower* chance of happening than other things that people should be *more* afraid of. Here are some annual U.S. statistics from that article:

28 Shark attacks vs. 4.5 million dog bites

321 Fatal airline accidents vs. 34,017 fatal car accidents

14,180 Murders vs. 33,289 suicides

40,170 Women who die from breast cancer vs. 432,709 women who die from cardiovascular disease

Source: *Newsweek*, April 2010

READ

 CD2, Track 16

1. Instruct students to read the stories.

2. Play the audio and have students follow along.

▶ *Reading and Writing 1, page 192*

MAIN IDEAS (5 minutes)

1. Read the directions aloud.

2. Ask students to read and complete the activity individually.

3. Ask for volunteers to share their answers and ask them to use evidence from the story to support their answers.

Main Idea Answers, p. 192
1. b; **2.** a; **3.** b; **4.** a

▶ *Reading and Writing 1, page 193*

DETAILS (10 minutes)

A (10 minutes)

1. Direct students to read the statements and complete the activity.

2. Have students compare answers with a partner.

3. Direct the students to look back at the stories to check their answers.

4. Go over the answers with the class.

Details Answers, p. 193
1. T; **2.** T; **3.** T; **4.** F; **5.** T; **6.** F

B (10 minutes)

1. Have students scan the reading, complete the activity, and compare answers with a partner.

2. Direct the students to look back at the stories to check their answers.

3. Go over the answers with the class.

Details Answers, p. 193
Answers will vary. Possible answers:
Facts: In 2005, 17.5 million people died of heart disease. Fewer than 300 people have ever died from mad cow disease.
Opinions: Doctors believe people can fight heart disease. We probably don't know anyone who had bird flu.

 For additional practice with reading comprehension, have students visit *Q Online Practice*.

WHAT DO YOU THINK?

A (15 minutes)

1. Ask students to read the questions and reflect on their answers.

2. Seat students in small groups and assign roles: a group leader to make sure everyone contributes, a note-taker to record the group's ideas, a reporter to share the group's ideas with the class, and a timekeeper to watch the clock.

3. Give students five minutes to discuss the questions. Call time if conversations are winding down. Allow them an extra minute or two if necessary.

> **Activity A Answers, pp. 193–194**
> Answers will vary.

▶ *Reading and Writing 1, page 194*

B (10 minutes)

1. Tell students that they should think about both Reading 1 and Reading 2 as they answer the questions in B.

2. Call on students to share their ideas with the class.

> **Activity B Answers, p. 194**
> Answers will vary.

MULTILEVEL OPTION

For B, have lower-level students write out some of their answers before they tell them to the group. Have higher-level students review and correct the statements as needed. Encourage one or two higher-level students to lead the class discussion.

Learning Outcome

Use the learning outcome to frame the purpose and relevance of Readings 1 and 2. Ask: *What did you learn from Reading 2 that prepares you to describe an unreasonable fear and explain how it can be avoided?*

Vocabulary Skill: Word families (5 minutes)

1. Ask a volunteer to read the introduction to word families aloud. Elicit/provide additional word families and/or words.

2. Check comprehension: *What is a word family? How are word families helpful to someone learning another language?*

Skill Note

In 2000, Dr. Averil Coxhead compiled 570 word families that occur quite often in academic texts. Each family has a "headword." Learning headwords, or one word in a word family, help uncover the meaning of other words in the family. Students already know the strategy of decoding new vocabulary. They should also be encouraged to see if they can associate an unfamiliar vocabulary word with a familiar word family. For example, if they know *familiar*, they have a shortcut to understanding words such as *familiarize* and *familiarity*. Helping students make these connections between words can reduce the time that students need to process new vocabulary—thus increasing their reading speed and honing their reading skills.

▶ *Reading and Writing 1, page 195*

A (5 minutes)

1. Direct students to work with a partner to complete the chart. Make sure you have enough dictionaries for students to use.

2. Go over the answers with the class.

> **Activity A Answers, p. 195**
> **2.** violence, [no verb], violent, violently;
> **3.** belief, believe, believable, believably;
> **4.** endangerment, endanger, endangered, [no adverb];
> **5.** harm, harm, harmful, harmfully;
> **6.** safety, [no verb], safe, safely

B (10 minutes)

1. Direct students to work on their own to complete each sentence. Have them check their answers with a partner.

2. Check answers as a class. Ask students to say the part of speech of each answer.

> **Activity B Answers, p. 195**
> **1.** fear
> **2.** safe
> **3.** violently
> **4.** violence
> **5.** danger
> **6.** safely
> **7.** fear

 For additional practice with word families, have students visit *Q Online Practice*.

An important 21st century skill is understanding that creativity and problem-solving processes progress over time. Success doesn't happen overnight. Setbacks occur, along with small successes, as people move toward their larger goals. Reaching these goals involves a long-term investment, patience, and a willingness to work through failure.

Practice this realization by asking students to reflect on the successes in their lives and note the small failures and successes that came before they reached their overarching goal. Have students share their stories with each other by writing or speaking. Tell your own story. What was your path to success? How did you find the strength to meet your goals despite failure? What are your current goals?

As this is the last unit, take this opportunity to encourage students to continue with their English-learning goals despite setbacks, despite challenges. Explain to them that perseverance is required for anyone who wants to accomplish their goals and dreams.

WRITING

▶ *Reading and Writing 1 page 196*

Writing Skill: Contrasting ideas with *however* (5 minutes)

1. Ask two higher-level students to read the introduction and examples.

2. Write the two example sentences for the first bullet on the board: *Crime rates are going down. However, most people think there is more crime.* Use this example to explain the first rule—However *usually comes at the beginning*…. Modify the example sentence as you progress through explaining the second and third rules.

3. Check comprehension: *What does* however *do? What three locations can* however *appear in a sentence? Do we need to use a comma with* however? *Why do we use the word* however?

4. Ask a higher-level student to summarize information about the use of the word *however* that the class just discussed.

A (10 minutes)

1. Read the directions aloud and go over the example. Direct students to complete the activity individually.

2. When finished, they should check their answers with a partner.

3. Go over the answers as a class.

Activity A Answers, pp. 196–197
2. a. We like to watch violent TV shows, but violence makes us anxious. b. We like to watch violent TV shows. However, violence makes us anxious;
3. a. I am more likely to die in a car accident, but I fear an airplane crash more. b. I am more likely to die in a car accident. However, I fear an airplane crash more;
4. a. Women fear crime more than men, but crime happens more often to men. b. Women fear crime more than men. However, crime happens more often to men;
5. a. Most crimes are not violent, but television focuses on the unusual and violent crimes. b. Most crimes are not violent. However, television focuses on the unusual and violent crimes.

▶ *Reading and Writing 1 page 197*

B (5 minutes)

1. Read the directions aloud. Rewrite the first one together.

2. Tell students to write sentences to complete the activity.

Activity B Answers, p. 197
Answers will vary. Possible answers:
2. Violence makes us anxious, however.;
3. I, however, fear an airplane crash more.;
4. Crime, however, happens more often to men.;
5. Television focuses on the unusual and violent crimes, however.

 For additional practice with contrasting ideas with *however*, have students visit *Q Online Practice*.

MULTILEVEL OPTION

Pair lower-level students with higher-level students. Have pairs create two or three more pairs of sentences for Activity A (e.g., *I am afraid of the ocean. I like swimming for exercise*). Once each pair has created two or three pairs of sentences, have pairs switch sentences. Then each pair should combine the sentences with *but* or *however* as they did in Activity A.

▶ Reading and Writing 1 page 198

Grammar:
Comparative adjectives (10 minutes)

1. Read the first sentence of the grammar point aloud. Ask for volunteers to read the sample sentences. Then present each bulleted point and supply/elicit additional examples.

2. Check comprehension by asking questions: *How is a comparative adjective different than a regular adjective? What's a syllable? What's the rule for two syllable adjectives that end in y? What's the rule for one syllable adjectives? How do you make* high *into a comparative adjective?* Large? Heavy? Beautiful?

3. Provide students with several different adjectives (e.g., *blue, big, hairy, hard, difficult*) and have students, in pairs, turn them into comparative adjectives.

4. For more practice with comparative adjectives, do the following Skill Note activity with your students.

Skill Note

Comparative adjectives are quite common in English—and sometimes difficult for students to master. Thus, practice makes perfect. Consider the following activities for your classroom:
1) Bring in items such as stuffed animals, fruit, pens, balls, books, or other items that can easily be compared. Have students make statements about the items in comparison to each other. Consider supplying sample adjectives that cover the adjective forms. For example, *The bear is bigger than the rabbit. The tennis ball is lighter than the basketball.*
2) Put students in groups of two or three and have them write sentences about each other using comparative adjectives. For example: *Diego is taller than me. Saida is younger than Tyrion.* Ensure that students create positive statements about each other.
3) Have students go outside and write sentences about things they see on campus or in the school, using comparative adjectives. For example: *The trees are greener than the grass. Room 23 is more energetic than Room 22.*

▶ Reading and Writing 1 page 199

A (10 minutes)

1. Review the directions with the class. Check comprehension by reviewing the answer to the first item.

2. Have students complete the rest of the chart individually. When complete, students should reviews answers with a partner.

3. Elicit and confirm answers as a class.

Activity A Answers, p. 199
1. more afraid **2.** bigger; **3.** more careful;
4. more dangerous; **5.** easier; **6.** newer;
7. more reasonable; **8.** safer; **9.** smarter;
10. more violent

B (10 minutes)

1. Tell students to read the directions silently and write their answers.

2. When finished, they should read their sentences to a partner and listen to their partner's sentences.

Activity B Answers, p. 199
1. Heart disease is more common than mad cow disease.;
2. I believe that flying is more dangerous than driving.;
3. I think crime dramas are scarier than real life.;
4. The crime rate in Canada in 2007 is lower than the crime rate in Canada 15 years ago.

▶ Reading and Writing 1, page 200

Q Unit Assignment:
Write one or more paragraphs about an unreasonable fear

Unit Question (5 minutes)

Refer students back to the ideas they discussed at the beginning of the unit about what they are afraid of. Bring out the posters made for Activity B in Preview the Unit. Cue students if necessary by asking specific questions about the content of the unit: *What things did we discuss that cause people to be afraid? What makes you afraid? What do you do to stay safe when you feel afraid? How does TV news make people feel afraid?* Read the direction lines for the assignment together to ensure understanding.

Learning Outcome

1. Tie the Unit Assignment to the unit learning outcome. Say: *The outcome for this unit is to describe an unreasonable fear and explain how it can be avoided. This Unit Assignment is going to let you show your skill in writing a paragraph about an unreasonable fear and how it can be avoided.*

2. Explain that you are going to use a rubric similar to their Self-Assessment checklist on p. 202 to grade their Unit Assignment. You can also share a copy of the Unit Assignment Rubric (on p. 108 of this *Teacher's Handbook*) with the students.

Plan and Write

Brainstorm

A (5 minutes)

Read the directions aloud. Direct students to brainstorm. Call time when it appears that most students are finished.

▶ *Reading and Writing 1, page 201*

Plan

B (10 minutes)

Ask for a volunteer to read the directions aloud. Remind students that the Unit Assignment is a good place for them to practice using the new vocabulary and grammar skills they have learned in this unit. Direct students to complete the sentences.

Critical Thinking Tip (1 minute)

1. Read the Critical Thinking Tip aloud.
2. Remind students to work on developing their ideas before they complete writing assignments, be they for school or in the workplace.

Critical Q: Expansion Activity

Develop Ideas

1. Have students write a response to the following question: *Why is fear sometimes a good thing?* Before they write, have them outline their ideas using graphic organizers or outlining skills presented in earlier units. Have them clearly write topic sentences and main ideas. Explain to them that someone else will write a paragraph based upon their notes, so they must develop their ideas clearly.

2. Ask students to trade their completed outlines or graphic organizers with a partner. Have students write a short paragraph using their partner's notes. Remind students that in order for their partners to write a successful paragraph, they will have to develop their ideas clearly and specifically in their outlines.

3. Have students turn in paragraphs and graphic organizers/outlines to you. Assess the final product and share your thoughts about the work the students did (positive and constructive comments) during the next class session.

Write

C (15 minutes)

As students complete B, direct them to silently read the directions for C and complete the activity.

Alternative Unit Assignments

Assign or have students choose one of these assignments to do instead of, or in addition to, the Unit Assignment.

1. Watch two news programs for three nights in a row. Take notes on the types of stories in each news program. Write down the number of these kinds of stories on each program:

   violent crime stories

   natural disaster stories

   stories about the economy

   stories about politics

   human interest stories

   What is each news program focusing on? Write a paragraph comparing the kinds of stories the two programs report.

2. Write a paragraph in which you give an opinion about a dangerous place (e.g., a dangerous section of your town or city, dark alleys) or situation (e.g., walking home from school at night) in your city or neighborhood.

    For an additional unit assignment, have students visit *Q Online Practice*.

Your Writing Process (1 minute)

1. Read the Your Writing Process tip aloud.
2. Encourage students to use *Q Online Practice* frequently.

Revise and Edit

Peer Review

A (10 minutes)

1. Pair students and direct them to read each other's work.

2. Ask students to answer the questions and discuss them.

3. Give students suggestions of helpful feedback: *Do we need to use a comma with* however? *Where does the comma go? That fear doesn't seem unreasonable; can you think of a more unreasonable fear? Your paragraph is about people, not about you. Can you change the paragraph so that it is about you? Can you include a few comparative adjectives in your paragraph?*

Rewrite

B (15–20 minutes)

Students should review their partners' answers from A and rewrite their paragraphs if necessary.

▶ *Reading and Writing 1, page 202*

Edit

C (15–20 minutes)

1. Direct students to read and complete the Self-Assessment checklist. They should be prepared to hand in their work or discuss it in class.

2. Ask for a show of hands for how many students gave all or mostly *Yes* answers.

3. Use the Unit Assignment Rubric on p. 108 in this *Teacher's Handbook* to score each student's assignment.

4. Alternatively, divide the class into large groups and have students read their paragraphs to their group. (Make copies of each student's writing for each person in the group, to assist with scoring.) Pass out copies of the Unit Assignment Rubric and have students grade each other.

▶ *Reading and Writing 1, page 203*

Track Your Success (5 minutes)

1. Have students circle the words they have learned in this unit. Suggest that students go back through the unit to review any words they have forgotten.

2. Have students check the skills they have mastered. If students need more practice to feel confident about their proficiency in a skill, point out the pages numbers and encourage them to review.

3. Read the learning outcome aloud (*Describe an unreasonable fear and explain how it can be avoided*). Ask students if they feel that they have met the outcome.

Unit Assignment Rubric

Student name: _____

Date: _____

Unit Assignment: *Write one or more paragraphs about an unreasonable fear.*

20 = Writing element was completely successful (at least 90% of the time).
15 = Writing element was mostly successful (at least 70% of the time).
10 = Writing element was partially successful (at least 50% of the time).
　0 = Writing element was not successful.

Writing One or More Paragraphs	20 points	15 points	10 points	0 points
Sentences have both a subject and a verb and those elements agree.				
The first line of each paragraph is indented, and sentences begin with capital letters and end with appropriate punctuation.				
The student clearly describes his/her fear and why it is unreasonable.				
Sentences use comparative adjectives correctly.				
Sentences contrast ideas with *however* correctly.				

Total points: _____

Comments:

Welcome to the Q Testing Program

1. MINIMUM SYSTEM REQUIREMENTS[1]

1024 x 768 screen resolution displaying 32-bit color

Web browser[2]:
Windows®-requires Internet Explorer® 7 or above
Mac®-requires OS X v10.4 and Safari® 2.0 or above
Linux®-requires Mozilla® 1.7 or Firefox® 1.5.0.9 or above

To open and use the customizable tests you must have an application installed that will open and edit .doc files, such as Microsoft® Word® (97 or higher).

To view and print the Print-and-go Tests, you must have an application installed that will open and print .pdf files, such as Adobe® Acrobat® Reader (6.0 or higher).

2. RUNNING THE APPLICATION

Windows®/Mac®
- Ensure that no other applications are running.
- Insert the Q: Skills for Success Testing Program CD-ROM into your CD-ROM drive.
- Double click on the file "start.htm" to start.

Linux®
- Insert the Q: Skills for Success Testing Program CD-ROM into your CD-ROM drive.
- Mount the disk on to the desktop.
- Double click on the CD-ROM icon.
- Right click on the icon for the "start.htm" file and select to "open with Mozilla".

3. TECHNICAL SUPPORT

If you experience any problems with this CD-ROM, please check that your machine matches or exceeds the minimum system requirements in point 1 above and that you are following the steps outlined in point 2 above.

If this does not help, e-mail us with your query at: elt.cdsupport.uk@oup.com
Be sure to provide the following information:

- Operating system (e.g. Windows 2000, Service Pack 4)
- Application used to access content, and version number
- Amount of RAM
- Processor speed
- Description of error or problem
- Actions before error occurred
- Number of times the error has occurred
- Is the error repeatable?

---

[1] The Q Testing Program CD-ROM also plays its audio files in a conventional CD player.

[2] Note that when browsing the CD-ROM in your Web browser, you must have pop-up windows enabled in your Web browser settings.

The Q Testing Program

The disc on the inside back cover of this book contains both ready-made and customizable versions of **Reading and Writing** and **Listening and Speaking** tests. Each of the tests consists of multiple choice, fill-in-the-blanks/sentence completion, error correction, sentence reordering/sentence construction, and matching exercises.

Creating and Using Tests

1. Select "Reading and Writing Tests" or "Listening and Speaking Tests" from the main menu.
2. Select the appropriate unit test or cumulative test (placement, midterm, or final) from the left-hand column.
3. For ready-made tests, select a Print-and-go Test, Answer Key, and Audio Script (for Listening and Speaking tests).
4. To modify tests for your students, select a Customizable Test, Answer Key, and Audio Script (for Listening and Speaking tests). Save the file to your computer and edit the test using Microsoft Word or a compatible word processor.
5. For Listening and Speaking tests, use the audio tracks provided with the tests. **Audio files for the listening and speaking tests can also be played in a standard CD player.**

Reading and Writing Tests

Each test consists of 40 questions taken from the selected unit. The Reading and Writing Tests assess reading skills, vocabulary, vocabulary skills, grammar, and writing skills.

Listening and Speaking Tests

Each test consists of 40 questions taken from the selected unit. The Listening and Speaking Tests assess listening skills, vocabulary, vocabulary skills, grammar, pronunciation, and speaking skills.

Cumulative Tests

The placement tests for both Listening and Speaking and Reading and Writing consist of 50 questions. Each placement test places students in the correct level of Q: Introductory–5. **A printable User Guide to help you administer the placement test is included with the placement test files on the CD-ROM.**

The midterm tests for both Listening and Speaking and Reading and Writing consist of 25 questions covering Units 1–5 of the selected Level. The midterm Reading and Listening texts are new and not used in any other tests or student books.

The final tests for both Listening and Speaking and Reading and Writing consist of 25 questions covering Units 6–10 of the selected Level. The final Reading and Listening texts are new and not used in any other tests or student books.